CRACKING THE CODE TO CRYPTOCURRENCY INVESTMENTS

CRACKING THE CODE TO CRYPTOCURRENCY INVESTMENTS

A COMPREHENSIVE GUIDE TO CRYPTOCURRENCIES, BLOCKCHAIN, AND CRYPTO WALLETS

IAN ELLUL

Copyright © 2021 by Ian Ellul

All rights reserved.

No part of this book may be reproduced in any form or by any electronic or mechanical means, including information storage and retrieval systems, without written permission from the author, except for the use of brief quotations in a book review.

INTRODUCTION

Cryptocurrencies are popular nowadays. Bitcoin, one of the leading and most expensive cryptocurrencies, has been developing rapidly.

But what is Cryptocurrency? And why are so many people now turning to it as an investment?

Cryptocurrency is a digital currency that can be used to make payments without the need for a bank and with strong encryption. Users can store, send, and receive cryptocurrency through a digital wallet. The most commonly known cryptocurrency is Bitcoin, but there are many others, such as Ethereum and Litecoin.

As the number of people making transactions with Bitcoin increases around the world, various scammers may try to steal your hard-earned coins by taking advantage of your lack of knowledge in security measures.

Let us begin by defining cryptocurrency. Cryptocurrency is a type of digital currency used to exchange for goods and services. Unlike the traditional money we use, cryptocurrency does not have its own physical entity like a paper bill or an actual coin. The currency's value is based solely on its ability to be traded for products or services. As opposed to legal tender issued by sovereign nations, cryptocurrency is not backed by government regulation or policies. Because of this and cryptocurrencies' anonymous nature due to blockchain, some have used them as media of exchange in illegal transactions such as drug dealing, human trafficking, and arms.

However, this changes when you choose Bitcoin as your cryptocurrency of choice because Bitcoin payments are *anonymized* but they are NOT *anonymous*.

Here is the difference:

Anonymous transactions are untraceable. When you send someone else some anonymized money, it is impossible for anyone to trace back that transaction to either one of you.

Crypto note technology, on the other hand, 'mixes' your transaction with so many other transactions that it makes it almost impossible for anyone to determine which funds in particular were sent to whom. The mixed-up coins can be then used again by the random user or distributed of randomly again through a different mechanism called Ring Signature (RingCT). This practically breaks any chain of custody between sender and recipient and makes the transaction nearly anonymous.

Cryptocurrency can be broken down into three main components:

- **Currency:** This is the one that you will receive in

exchange for goods or services. If you do a BTC to USD transaction, the only thing you would receive is USD.
- **Exchange:** An online platform that allows users to exchange different currencies between each other using their own cryptocurrency.
- **Wallet:** A digital system that stores your cryptocurrency and allows you to send and receive them from others. The technology is also designed in a way that it is difficult to duplicate or falsify this data. Cryptography provides the basis for security functions of this technology.

Cryptocurrency, popularly known as "digital" or "virtual currency," is a part of the crypto-technology development, which has two main aspects to it. First, crypto-technology encompasses the actual development platform for technological innovation contributing to the creation of new financial products. In other words, the process by which technology is transformed into practical application. Second, it describes the community of crypto developers, engineers, programmers, coders, architects, and consultants engaged in the application of top-end solutions and blockchain engineering and cryptocurrency development. All of this will change money the way the internet changed how we access information.

Despite the naysayers, cryptocurrency has already gained legitimacy as a financially viable commodity throughout the world. One of my favorite benefits about using cryptocurrency is that it avoids overpaying for currency conversion fees while making international business transactions as long as it is kept within the cryptocurrency environment. So currently if one converts from fiat to crypto there are brokerage charges as with any other such transactions. But this is not so when one makes transactions with a cryptocurrency of choice such as Bitcoin within the crypto environment.

Today, as I write hundreds of restaurants in the US as well as the UK and other countries accept bitcoin using QR scanners directly from your virtual wallet. These establishments indicate in their store windows or website that they accept BTC payments. eCommerce platforms such as Shopify used to setup online stores, nearly 100,000 merchants accept bitcoin payments. Overstock through which purchases of furniture, jewelry, clothes and much more with bitcoin are also accepted. You can pay for your flights and hotels with bitcoin via Expedia, Bitcoin.travel and Cheapoair. Dish Network accepts bitcoin for home installations satellite TV, Amazon Alexa as well as other products and services. Online casinos and sportsbooks also accept bitcoin. Microsoft and Dell have also joined the party. And with Gift Cards one can purchase gift cards with bitcoin via their eGifter.com tool. Hence cryptocurrency is already in use as an efficient alternative to digitalized fiat money payment systems globally.

These are just some of the many advantages that cryptocurrency has, but what if I told you that you can protect your money from being stolen by using something as simple as your cell phone?

Crypto Wallet is a mobile application that aims to

provide effective protection of your cryptocurrency by allowing you to store it in an encrypted form. The app allows you to be able to make transactions with the currency then reverts it back into account or into cash when you need. In addition, Crypto Wallet also offers 24/7 customer service and secure payment features.

The Crypto Wallet application is designed to provide users with a safe, secure, and convenient method of storing their cryptocurrencies. The Blockchain technology used in the application ensures that all your transactions are fast, direct, and secure, regardless of where you are in the world. The handy app allows you to send, receive, and view your cryptocurrency balance from anywhere at any time.

Crypto Wallet is a mobile application that runs on Android devices and is designed with iOS users in mind as well. The app is available in the Google Play Store and the Apple App Store. It can be downloaded for free, but there is a monthly subscription fee to be able to use it.

Cryptocurrency is a decentralized system of payment which exists exclusively in digital form, and as such, susceptible to many Internet threats. Crypto Wallet eliminates those threats by using advanced encryption technology with blockchain security methods and other server cluster node technologies. The application allows you to be able to protect your cryptocurrency from unauthorized access via encryption to verify transactions. This means advanced coding is involved in storing and transmitting cryptocurrency data between wallets and to public ledgers. In the background, a crypto wallet stores a private key, which is a secure digital code known only to the owner.

This private key **is** the 'connection' between you, the owner, and a public key, or a series of public keys (numeric codes associated with a certain number of Bitcoins). The encrypted data is stored on highly secure servers available 24/7 in multiple locations around the world. Security can be further enhanced by choosing a hardware wallet which are USB-like devices which come with pre-installed security layers to keep the private key safe within a certified secure chip.

Why do People Turn to Cryptocurrency?

It is undeniable that many people chose to use the cryptocurrency for their payment and investment because of the following reasons:

You have better control over your money. When you use cryptocurrency, it is not stored in a physical form. As its name suggests, there's just a digital record of your coins, and you don't have to worry about losing your money from physical damage or theft as long as your private key is safe as we already mentioned above.

No intermediaries between users and their money. The transactions made through cryptocurrencies are direct, peer-to-peer transactions, which means no bank or any other financial institution is involved in the process. This also means that there's no need for these financial institutions to earn high fees on international transactions. It is worth mentioning that cryptocurrencies are created by a competitive and decentralized process called mining. In other words cryptos are the reward to such miners by the network for their services in the form of transaction processing as well as network securing using specialized hardware to collect bitcoins in exchange.

It is affordable. Cryptocurrency utilizes blockchain technology, which ensures that all transactions are safe and secure. This is because blockchain comes with a number of built-in security features. Being in and of itself a peer-to-peer networked database which is governed by a set of rules. This is a shift towards transparency from traditional trust agents, in the process of tracking and auditing digital assets by incentivizing the validation of transactions for tamperproof record keeping. Governments are developing blockchain based systems and it is predicted that by 2024 the global blockchain market will be worth over US$ 20 billion.

Investing in Cryptocurrency

Those are some of the many benefits of using cryptocurrency. The emergence of cryptocurrency has opened up a lot of financial opportunities for people who are interested in investing.

What exactly is investing?

Investing is simply the act of committing money or capital in order to gain profit from it in the future. Investing can be done through lots of channels, but I am going to discuss only two financial instruments:

Traditional Investments: Some investment channels, such as stocks, bonds, EFTs etc. require you either use your bank account and credit card or pay cash. Some people like physical cash and feel confident holding it. That's fine, but it doesn't get you very far when you're looking at long-term investing. After all, if you had $50 in cash in your hand one day and two months later it's only worth $45 because of inflation, you may have lost a substantial amount of money compared to someone who invested that same amount in the stock market and had it grow to $55 over the same period of time.

Cryptocurrency Investments: With the rise of cryptocurrency, there is now another alternative that offers similar profit potential but with many advantages over traditional investments. Firstly cryptos are not like traditional money as due to their limited nature they are not affected by inflation which creates bubbles ruining financial markets. Also, middlemen are not used so transactions are easier and faster with no additional transaction fees. Transactions with cryptos are therefore confidential and have the potential to help the unbanked among us. International exchanges for business people are made without complications and added fees. As the network is in control, rather than any central power such governments or banks, it is not farfetched to countenance a scenario where banks as we know them now cease to exist. While cryptos are not subject to inflation as fiat money is, the fact is that with bitcoin for example the number of new bitcoins created yearly is automatically halved and will be halted when twenty-one million bitcoins have been created. Cryptos have both the usefulness and characteristics of money, such as durability, recognizability, portability and divisibility, meaning these currencies are based on mathematics rather than physical properties as with gold and silver. Therefore cryptos will increasingly hold value as trust and adoption increases. This can already be measured by the growing number of users, merchants, and startups. At the end of the day, as with any currency, the value of cryptos comes directly from people willing to accept them as payment.

How Do I Invest in Cryptocurrency?

Investing in cryptocurrency is easier than you think, even if you're an absolute beginner... and it's also risk-free! How so? This book will guide you. Let us begin.

1 / INTRODUCTION TO CRYPTOCURRENCY

THE GOAL of this chapter is to give a brief introduction to what cryptocurrency is, its history, and the different applications it can have in our lives. You will also learn the difference between Bitcoin and Ethereum.

WHAT IS CRYPTOCURRENCY?

Cryptocurrency (aka "altcoins" or "crypto") was invented in 2009 by an unknown person using the alias Satoshi Nakamoto. This currency is decentralized (i.e., not issued by any government), encrypted (i.e., not easily forged), and uses a public ledger where all transactions are recorded (known as a blockchain). In the case of Bitcoin, it is not possible to exceed the limit of twenty-one million Bitcoins that can exist in the system. This is an advantage because it eliminates inflation.

Launched in 2009, Bitcoin was the first successful cryptocurrency to hold increasing trust and popular adoption, but there are now many others such as Ethereum. The code for Ethereum was written by a developer or group of developers using the name Vitalik Buterin, and it launched in 2015.

As a note, some prefer to use the term "digital currency" instead of cryptocurrency (though digital currency can mean electronic money that is used online). In order to participate in the cryptocurrency ecosystem, one has to have a wallet on their computer cellphone or as a USB-based hardware device. People can choose to leave their wallets open for trading, or they can encrypt it. As with everything else in life you choose how secure or not your assets are. Users with encrypted wallets never have to provide their personal information when they are executing a transaction secured by private keys. A private key is a secret number that allows one to spend cryptos. The keys are mathematically related to all addresses generated for a given cryptocurrency within a wallet. These need to be kept safe and certified secured chips do just that These chips ensure that only public data is shared via Bluetooth but not private keys. Should the Bluetooth connection be hacked, these chips require your consent for the sharing of other data. Moreover, private keys consist of 256 bits which can be represented as a 32-bit hexadecimal key or 64 characters made of numbers and letters as shown here:

E9873D79C6D87DC0FB6A5778633389T_
F2253213303DB61F20BD67CC233AA33245

When an encrypted wallet is created, you're given a

public address, and this is considered your public-facing identity in the cryptocurrency system. This address has to be shown in order to send or receive money, but no other personal information needs to be revealed. This makes it hard for governments and hackers alike to know anything about you when dealing with cryptocurrencies.

In order to send or receive money, people have to have a public address and a private key. The public address the outward-facing identity code, and the private key is needed to identify the owner of the address. No one can spend money from someone else's address, because they do not have access to the private key. When sending or receiving cryptocurrency, you will need to know this information about the person on the other end. When paying for something at a store using cash (which doesn't require identification), you don't need to know any personal information about the cashier in order for him or her to give you your change back. This is not the case whenever you deal with cryptocurrency, which requires applying some of the same basic standards for any transaction.

Wallets come in two forms: software wallets (like Jaxx, Exodus, or Multibit) or online wallets (like hosted wallet services such as Blockchain.com). However, online wallets are not secure and can be hacked like any other computer; it would therefore be unwise for people to store a lot of money in an online wallet. A good rule of thumb is to keep only a little bit of money in an online wallet for trading. For convenience and ease of use, the other option is software wallets, which store your "private key" (i.e. the info that could identify you) on your computer or phone, therefore eliminating the need to trust an external service provider with your funds.

HOW DO I GET STARTED WITH CRYPTOCURRENCY?

When you first grab your Bitcoin wallet, a small amount of Bitcoin will be sent to it through a process called mining. Mining is the way that new Bitcoin is produced and transactions are processed. Miners (i.e., computers or nodes on the network) are responsible for confirming transactions and providing security to the network in return for newly created Bitcoin, as well as a small transaction fee paid by the user sending money.

This decentralized server process is how Bitcoin is created in the first place. As already mentioned, every cryptocurrency has a maximum cap on the number of coins which can be mined and brought into existence. Once this limit is there will not be any new coins mined or produced in any other way as the planet's supply will essentially be tapped out. At that point miners will be incentivized to process the associated transactions fees instead of the coins. It is however possible for a crypto's protocol to be changed by its creators to allow for a larger supply. The final bitcoin is expected to be mined around the year 2140.

The amount of Bitcoin that you will receive when you first create your wallet will be tiny (a few cents or less), but over time, you should see your balance gradually increase as more Bitcoins are sent to your wallet through mining. It can take a few days for the transaction to go through if it originates from a bank account. If you have an account at an exchange that has trading enabled or in a wallet that already contains some Bitcoin (or any other cryptocurrency), and you want to transfer some of this cryptocurrency to your newly-created wallet (e.g., for the purpose of making purchases), then there will generally be no wait time for the transaction to go through. If you are able to immediately transfer the amount of cryptocurrency that you want to your wallet, this might be a sign that the exchange or wallet service is not a safe place to store your funds.

SECURITY TIPS FOR THE AVERAGE USER

When storing digital currency on an exchange or online wallet service that holds your private key for you, it's important that you have a solid understanding of their security protocols. This is even more important if you are holding an amount of Bitcoin worth more than you could ever afford to lose. By following these security tips, even if there is a breach in security and your account details are stolen, there's a better chance that no harm will come from it.

1. Make sure you have the two-factor authentication feature enabled, also known as 2FA or 2SV. This means that when anyone logs into your account (even yourself), they will have to enter a security code in addition to your username and password. This code is usually texted to you when someone tries to log into your account, but it can also be generated by an app like Duo on your computer or phone. Not all cryptocurrency exchanges offer

2FA, so you might want to look for one that does if this feature is important to you.
2. Only keep enough currency in your exchange or online wallet that you are actively using and planning on using in the near future. The rest should be kept in a more secure location like a hardware wallet.
3. Avoid keeping your cryptocurrency holdings on one exchange or online wallet service. Move them to different wallets every few months, ideally at least once a year. This helps to make sure that if there is ever a breach in security, your entire portfolio is not wiped out (which might happen if you keep all of your coins in one place).
4. Use 2FA and any other security measures offered by the exchange or online wallet if possible.
5. Use a different password for each of your cryptocurrency accounts. Some exchanges let you add an additional layer of security by setting up a password hint question and answer that you have to enter when you log in, just in case you forget your password. Other services provide optional two-factor authentication using security software like the Google Authenticator app on your phone rather than text messages sent to your phone number.
6. Make sure that the exchange or online wallet has good customer service, especially if you're not an experienced user who is able to independently

verify the integrity of their security protocols yourself.

Whether you're using a cryptocurrency exchange, an online wallet service, or a desktop or mobile wallet created by the software development team behind your digital currency, make sure you know how to evaluate their reputation for security. The more secure your funds are, the better off you will be if there is ever a breach in security at that particular exchange or wallet.

Ready to get started? Let us delve more into cryptocurrency.

2 / BLOCKCHAIN TECHNOLOGY

WHAT IS BLOCKCHAIN TECHNOLOGY?

BLOCKCHAIN TECHNOLOGY IS the key to digital coins such as Bitcoin and is one of the most widely known applications of its kind. It allows us to have an online ledger that cannot be tampered with, and this makes it possible for transactions to happen in a way that seems much fairer than before.

To understand how Blockchain technology works, one must first grasp the concept of a database that cannot be tampered with. In the past, this was not possible. There were many factors that made it easy to subvert a database: physical tampering via hacking, or changing entries from within a network via an administrator account, which can have administrator privileges. These problems have been solved with Bitcoin's blockchain innovation because it is decentralized and distributed.

A database is "decentralized" if it is copied to many nodes and "distributed" if it is divided into multiple parts.

Bitcoin's blockchain technology is decentralized in that every node has an up-to-date copy of the ledger and distributed in that the ledger exists on every single node.

HOW DOES IT WORK?

The best way to understand this technology is by using a non-digital analogy: someone who wishes to change entries in a paper ledger book must get permission from all of the other parties involved. This would be impossible with a digital ledger because there are not enough people working at the same organization to ensure that the attacker was caught, which means that there would always be danger of fraud.

Blockchain solves this by giving every party a copy of the ledger and making their presence known to the network. Anyone who tries to modify the ledger's data will have to subvert all of the decentralized nodes in the system to maintain their privacy. It is not possible for someone to revert back to an old copy of the ledger because it is stored on every node in the network at once.

BLOCKCHAIN TECHNOLOGY AND CRYPTOCURRENCY

Blockchain technology is important when it comes to cryptocurrency because it solves the problem of double spending. Double spending is what happens when a person tries to send two conflicting transactions at the same time. This problem has been prevalent with digital currency for a long time, but Spondoolies-Tech Ltd

(OTCMKTS:SPLTF) has developed a solution to this issue. The SP20 was released by Spondoolies-Tech Ltd and was the first Bitcoin mining device that could mine Bitcoin and Litecoin at the same time. This created the Multi-Pool functionality, which made it possible for these miners to extract cryptocurrencies in different hashing algorithms without having multiple devices or switching between them manually. SP20 also had a new feature called the Dual-Path, which allowed it to mine both SHA-256 (the algorithm used by Bitcoin's Blockchain) and Scrypt (the algorithm used by Litecoin's).

HOW DO I TRUST BLOCKCHAIN TECHNOLOGY?

The security of a blockchain network depends on how many nodes are in the system. This is because the more nodes there are, the harder it is for someone to subvert them all. For example, if there are 100 nodes in a system and one of them is hacked, the attacker must subvert at least 51% of them to take control of the ledger. This makes it harder for someone to attack a system with many nodes than it would be with a few.

Bitcoin's Blockchain currently has more than 7,000 decentralized nodes, which means that it is very secure. The SP20 miners are helping secured Bitcoin's blockchain by mining Bitcoin at the same time as they mine Litecoin using SHA-256 or Scrypt algorithms. This means that there will be more mining power used against Bitcoin, and therefore, an attacker would need more power to gain control of the network with an attack in the future.

WHY USE A BLOCKCHAIN TO SECURE A DATABASE?

A blockchain is an unchangeable ledger because it has so many decentralized nodes, making data tampering nearly impossible. This means that it is useful for applications in which data integrity needs to be maintained. The SP20 miners are great examples of why this technology is important, as they are helping to maintain the safety of the Bitcoin and Litecoin blockchains.

WHAT ARE SOME OTHER USES FOR BLOCKCHAIN TECHNOLOGY?

Blockchain's transparency can be applied to many other areas of business, including credit card payments, stock trading, and music royalties. It also has the potential to be implemented in voting systems and land registry offices.

The technology is being developed each day by many start-ups, so we can expect that there will be new applications for it in the near future.

RECAP:

What are some other uses for Blockchain technology? — credit card payment processing, stock trading, and music royalties.

How does Blockchain technology work? — Blockchain

technology allows a decentralized database to be shared by multiple users.

How Do I Trust Blockchain Technology? — Your trust is based off of the number of nodes in your system.

Why use a blockchain to secure a database? — It makes it harder to modify data on a decentralized network since multiple parties are responsible for doing so.

3 / VARIOUS PLATFORMS FOR TRADING CRYPTOCURRENCY

PLATFORM FOR CRYPTOCURRENCY refers to the distribution of a blockchain network's computing power among the different users running a node. A typical cryptocurrency system will comprise two main components: nodes and blocks. *Nodes* maintain a record of transactions in each *block* and work to solve complex mathematical problems that help confirm legitimate transactions. These are often validated through consensus by other nodes in the network before becoming part of the blockchain (a chain of blocks). As nodes are being added to the network, they require connections to other nodes in order to communicate with the entire network and stay synchronized with one another. This has the result of distributing the overall network's combined hashrate equally among these nodes.

"Hashrate" refers to the combined computing power per second used to mine and process calculations in blockchain such as Bitcoin and is a fixed-length alphanumeric code used to represent either words, messages and data.

The real distribution of hashrate for most cryptocurrencies is unknown due to the efforts of individual miners to remain anonymous. However, researchers have attempted to estimate the real distribution and ecosystem effects from hashing power in cryptocurrency networks, as this can have an impact on whether or not transactions are made in a timely fashion. It can also be a factor that determines how efficiently networks will manage information processing demands.

The larger the network that is being created, the more difficult it becomes for any individual node to solve mathematical problems associated with transaction confirmation and record keeping. This can result in a bottleneck that can slow transactions and create bottlenecks for block creation. These issues have been further exacerbated in a system where miners must compete with one another to create new blocks and earn rewards or processing fees.

Example: In the case of Bitcoin, researchers at Cornell University discovered that this competition has resulted in the distribution of hashpower becoming increasingly centralized; from 80 percent in 2013 to less than 20 percent by 2017. This has created greater centralization with most mining power being concentrated among a small group of mining power companies. The reason for this is because mining rigs utilizing more efficient ASIC hardware have been difficult for individuals to acquire on their own, and require the resources of larger organizations.

The most practical solution to a network bottleneck is the expansion of the overall size of the blockchain network. This can be achieved by including more nodes in the network. However, this also involves overcoming some barriers in order to expand a blockchain's ecosystem.

There are other innovations that can help reduce network bottlenecks in cryptocurrency networks, such as creating systems that more evenly distribute transactions among nodes and prevent mining monopolies from developing (or at least limit their impact). Peernova introduced its hybrid Proof-of-Work/Proof-of-Stake (PoW/PoS) system, which gives users a greater ability to participate in consensus without requiring them to immediately own expensive hardware.

Here is a list of all the platforms that are currently in use for cryptocurrency. Some are more popular than others, but they're all worth exploring for yourself.

COINBASE

Coinbase is one of the first cryptocurrency exchanges and is still one of the most popular. It offers Bitcoin, Litecoin, Ethereum, and Bitcoin Cash trades in an intuitive user interface. Coinbase also offers a digital wallet that stores these coins securely on your phone or computer so you can spend them at any time without needing any kind of app or hardware device (just like a cash wallet). Once you decide which coins you want to invest in, Coinbase has relatively low fees on transactions to make buying/selling easy.

Coinbase does a good job of explaining the basics of Bitcoin and cryptocurrency in general. They also offer an easy-to-use app that allows you to send, receive, and store digital coins. Coinbase has a team of professional security experts who are constantly working on keeping your coins safe from hackers or other security breaches. You can put your coins in cold storage (offline) or use the Coinbase Vault for secure storage that you control. The vault is insured to protect users against any losses if Coinbase were to become insolvent.

Coinbase is based in San Francisco, California and adheres to US law while focusing on serving the whole world.

BITPANDA

Bitpanda is a European-based exchange that has a simple user interface that offers popular coins like Bitcoin, Ethereum, Ripple, Litecoin and Cardano. It supports payment methods like credit card and SEPA transfer. Bitpanda was founded in 2014 and has gained popularity with European traders.

CEX

CeX is another popular cryptocurrency exchange that supports credit card and bank transfers (via Bitcoin, Ripple, Ethereum, Bitcoin cash). CeX is a London-based company founded in 2013. It's the first cryptocurrency exchange to expand to multiple countries, as it's now available in the USA, Germany, South Korea, China and Russia. The company uses an advanced trading platform for reliable order execution that combines a trading engine with a matching engine for processing orders quickly. This allows users to enjoy faster execution of any trades while providing liquidity to the market at the same time. CeX has also been working to improve customer support by adding multilingual capabilities and chat features.

CeX has a relatively low 0.2% fee for all trades, and there are no deposit fees. The exchange supports major coins like Bitcoin, Ethereum, Bitcoin Cash, Ripple and Dash.

COINMAMA

Coinmama is another popular platform for buying cryptocurrency using your credit card or cash (via Western Union or MoneyGram). Coinmama is an Israel-based company founded in 2013 that supports buying BTC, ETH, LTC, XRP and DASH with credit or debit cards issued by Visa or MasterCard. Coinmama has relatively high fees compared to other exchanges that serve the U.S. market, but if you want to buy coins with cash or a credit card, there are few other choices and Coinmama is one of the most popular options.

Coinmama is a well-established cryptocurrency exchange platform founded in 2013 by Asher Tan. The company provides cryptocurrency trading services to more than 150 countries worldwide including the US, Canada, UK and many others. The platform also allows users to buy digital currencies using their debit cards or bank accounts with transaction fees starting from 2%.

KRAKEN

Kraken, around since 2011, is one of the oldest cryptocurrency exchanges with its headquarters in San Francisco, and it's one of the top 15 companies by daily trade volume. It supports EUR, USD, CAD and GBP in addition to Bitcoin, Ethereum and a wide range of other cryptocurrencies including Ripple, Litecoin and Zcash. Kraken has low fees (0% for market makers). Usual practice is for a trade order to get the maker fee if it did not match immediately against an order presently on the order book, which adds liquidity. To avoid this one ought to use the Post Limit Order option thus ensuring your order limit order will be charged the maker fee or be cancelled. Maker fees usually start at 0.16% and can go as low as 0% as with Kraken.

EXMO

EXMO is a UK-based and Russia-licensed cryptocurrency exchange that supports Bitcoin, Ethereum, Litecoin, and other major cryptocurrencies. The platform provides user support in English, Russian, Chinese and German. EXMO has low fees (0.2%) for all transactions on the exchange. The company has been serving customers since 2013.

EXMO is also one of the few exchanges that supports fiat currency (EUR) deposits and withdrawals via bank transfer along with credit/debit cards and e-wallets (Payeer, AdvCash, Neteller). EXMO also offers margin trading on a limited selection of cryptocurrencies like Bitcoin, Ethereum, Litecoin Dash and Zcash.

YOBIT

YoBit is a cryptocurrency exchange founded in Russia that supports BTC, POLY, ETH, ETC, USDT and RPX. The YoBit platform offers a fully customizable interface and allows users to create multiple accounts. It also provides a professional trading terminal for more experienced traders as well as an in-depth knowledge base with informational guides and tutorials.

YoBit was founded in 2015 and the team is based in Moscow, Russia. It has been growing steadily over the years, making it one of the top 50 exchanges overall with a daily trade volume of $15 Million USD (October 2017).

BITFINEX

Bitfinex is one of the world's largest cryptocurrency exchanges by trading volume. Founded in 2012, it's based in Hong Kong and currently handles around $1.5 Billion USD a day. Bitfinex offers trading on a large number of cryptocurrencies, along with leveraged margin trading and liquidity swaps.

Bitfinex has been hacked before (in 2016), but the company paid back customers from their own pockets to fully compensate them for their losses (like they did for all of the other big hacks that happened between 2015-2017).

KUCOIN

KuCoin is a newer cryptocurrency exchange platform that was founded in September 2017, but it's already managed to grow into one of the top 20 exchanges by trade volume and daily users. The exchange is based in Hong Kong, and it supports BTC, ETH, NEO, EOS and many other popular cryptocurrencies.

COINCORNER

CoinCorner is a cryptocurrency exchange founded on the Isle of Man,UK. The platform was launched in 2015, and it supports Bitcoin, Ethereum, Litecoin and Dogecoin purchases with direct bank deposits. CoinCorner provides user support in English and also offers a mobile app that can be downloaded from the Google Play store or App Store.

ITBIT

ItBit is a US-based regulated financial services company that provides trading services for digital currencies such as Bitcoin (BTC), Ether (ETH) & Litecoin (LTC). It also offers data reporting services for financial institutions that are required by law to produce them.

ItBit was founded in 2012 and is based in New York City, USA. It also offers an online browser-based trading platform for its customers to trade, buy and sell digital currencies. The business has been rising steadily since it started and became one of the largest cryptocurrency exchanges in the world with a day-to-day trade volume of $103 Million USD (November 2017).

GEMINI

Gemini is a New York-based digital currency exchange that was launched by the Winklevoss twins (the infamous brothers involved in early Facebook) back in 2015. It supports BTC and ETH trading along with other major cryptocurrencies like Litecoin, Zcash etc. The platform provides user support in English and is on mobile platforms like Android and iOS devices.

COINFLOOR

Coinfloor is a UK-based cryptocurrency exchange that was founded in 2013 by Mark Lamb and Tim Rehder. It supports GBP only as the fiat currency and also supports quite a few cryptocurrencies including: BTC, BCH, ETH, LTC, XRP, and DASH. The company has been growing steadily during its short lifespan (4 years), and it became one of the main cryptocurrency exchanges in Europe with a daily trade volume of $72 Million USD (November 2017).

QUOINEX

Quoinex is an established cryptocurrency exchange platform founded in 2014 by Mike Kayamori in Japan. The platform provides users with access to multiple cryptocurrencies including BTC, BCH, ETH etc. as well as serves corporate customers like Overstock Japan and Bloomberg.com. The has been growing steadily since it started. It has a daily trade volume of $65 Million USD (November 2017).

4 / BEST PRACTICES

WHEN DEALING WITH CRYPTOCURRENCIES, you should always make sure to use the best practices to ensure you're keeping your funds safe. This includes practicing the following:

BACKUP YOUR WALLETS IN A SAFE PLACE

You should make sure to keep a backup of your wallet details somewhere safe — otherwise, you risk losing everything if your computer breaks or the hard drive gets damaged. It's also important to make sure that the location where you keep your backup is safe from natural disasters and other issues, and that it isn't vulnerable to fire or theft.

UPDATE SOFTWARE REGULARLY

You should always ensure you are using the latest version of any software related to your cryptocurrency holdings, including wallet software and mining clients. Out-of-date software can be compromised. You should always keep up to date with all security patches for the software you are using, as well as operating system updates.

PROTECT YOUR COMPUTER

Cybercriminals will always be looking for ways to infiltrate your computer, so you should make sure to use strong security measures. In particular, you should always make sure that you regularly run up-to-date anti-virus software and a firewall. You should also create strong passwords and avoid connecting your computer to public networks or untrusted networks.

KEEP BACKUPS OF FILES ON PAPER

If you want to keep a backup of any information related to your cryptocurrency holdings — including private keys, the encryption seed, logins or passwords — it's worth making sure that you keep redundant backups in at least two different locations.

USE TWO-FACTOR AUTHENTICATION

When using exchanges or online wallets, it's important to ensure that you are using two factor authentications (2FA) whenever possible. It's also a good idea to turn on 2FA on any other accounts related to your cryptocurrency holdings, including email accounts and social media accounts. Even if someone steals your password, they won't be able to access your account if you have 2FA enabled.

LOOK FOR WEBSITES THAT ARE SECURE BY DESIGN

You should always check that the site you are using is secure; otherwise, you could find yourself vulnerable to hackers and cybercriminals. The site should have the HTTPS protocol with a secure certificate — and this should be displayed in the address bar. It's worth double checking that the site is encrypted — and there should be a padlock icon at the bottom of your browser window. It's also worth checking that the site isn't asking for any unnecessary information from you, or requesting personal details that could be used to access your cryptocurrency holdings.

KEEP MULTIPLE SECURE COPIES OF YOUR BACKUP

Make sure the one offline copy stored in a bank deposit box or similar location. If you are going to be moving large amounts of money, it's recommended that you keep a backup in at least 3 secure locations. One should be on your computer (or on a USB stick that is not connected to the internet), another on a private server, and the last one offline, such as in a bank deposit box.

USE VPNS FOR ALL ONLINE ACTIVITY

You should use a VPN when working with any cryptocurrency, as this adds an extra layer of security for your online transactions — and also allows you to remain anonymous. This is especially important if you are doing any trading using an exchange or wallet that isn't directly linked to your financial details.

USE STRONG PASSWORDS THAT ARE UNIQUE FOR EACH ACCOUNT AND SITE YOU VISIT

You should use strong, unique passwords for each of your cryptocurrency accounts. This will help to ensure that you don't end up with a situation where one compromise leads to the compromise of multiple accounts. It's also important to make sure that the passwords are long and complex enough — ideally, passwords should be at least 8 characters long and include upper- and lower-case letters, as well as numbers and symbols.

CHANGE ALL YOUR PASSWORDS REGULARLY, AT LEAST EVERY 90 DAYS

Changing your passwords regularly will help to avoid situations where a compromise could lead to your password being used for nefarious purposes. If you receive any emails asking for personal information, or if your computer displays any alerts related to malware or security issues, it's also important that you change all of your passwords as soon as possible.

USE DECOY WALLETS

If you find yourself in a situation where someone has access to one of your wallets, it's possible that they may try to steal the funds in the wallet. This is especially true if the wallet belongs to an exchange, and contains a large amount of money — so you should always have at least one "decoy" wallet on each platform where you store funds.

USE AN ENCRYPTED PASSWORD MANAGER TO HELP MANAGE YOUR PASSWORDS

This is an effective way to help make sure you have strong and unique passwords for each of your cryptocurrency accounts. The best 5 password managers at the moment are Dashline, NordPass, RoboForm, 1Password, and Keeper.

BE CAREFUL WITH SOCIAL MEDIA, AS SOME PROFILES MAY BE FRAUDULENT

If you are posting information related to your cryptocurrency holdings on social media, it's important that you double check the account is legitimate before sharing any sensitive information — especially if the profile has been created in a hurry or seems like a fake. It's also worth double checking any links provided by the account, as these may lead to compromised websites.

AVOID USING GENERIC PASSWORDS

You should avoid using generic passwords that are easy to guess, such as "qwerty" or "password," on any accounts related to your cryptocurrency holdings, including email and social media accounts. This is to avoid a situation where a compromised account could lead to the compromise of multiple accounts.

AVOID USING PHONES OR COMPUTERS THAT ARE USED BY OTHER PEOPLE

This should be a general rule for any technology you use — but avoiding the use of shared devices will help to make sure that your private keys and credentials are not compromised by hackers. It's important that you take full control over your devices, making sure that they are encrypted with strong passwords, and that all software is kept up to date. Never leave cryptocurrency wallets on public PCs and/or devices, as these may be subject to malware and/or keylogger attacks designed to steal private keys and login credentials.

CREATE AN IDEA OF HOW MUCH TOTAL USD VALUE IS STORED ON ALL ACCOUNTS AT ANY GIVEN TIME

If you have several different cryptocurrency accounts, you should practice creating an idea of how much total USD value is stored in all of your accounts at any given time. This will help to detect any suspicious activity in real-time, should it occur.

IF YOUR PRIVATE KEY HAS BEEN COMPROMISED, TRANSFER YOUR FUNDS TO A NEW ADDRESS IMMEDIATELY

If your private key has been compromised, it's possible that attackers may try to access the wallet and take the money stored within it. For this reason, it's important that if you believe that your account may be at risk of being compromised, you should make sure to transfer the funds to a new address as soon as possible.

NEVER LEAVE CRYPTOCURRENCY FUNDS ON EXCHANGES OR OTHER PLATFORMS WITHOUT CREATING A WITHDRAWAL WALLET FIRST

If you want to store your funds on an exchange, it's best to keep only the amount of funds you need to use for trading on the exchange itself.

Due to the high risk of exchange hacks and exit scams, it's recommended that you create a withdrawal wallet outside of an exchange before depositing any funds from your main wallet. This can be done by transferring cryptocurrency to a different wallet address where you have exclusive control over the private key, or by moving cryptocurrency into a paper storage solution (e.g., physical hardware wallets).

NEVER SUBMIT YOUR PRIVATE KEY OR RECOVERY PHRASES FOR ANY REASON

If you end up signing up to an exchange, cryptocurrency trading platform, or other cryptocurrency service, many of them will ask you to submit your private key and recovery phrase so that they can help recover your account if it becomes compromised. Please note that this is completely unnecessary as these service providers have no reason to help you if your account gets hacked since they would not be able to get the stolen funds back from the hackers themselves anyway.

Never submit your private keys or recovery phrase (used to regenerate your keys should a ledger goes out of business or its hardware device lost) for any reason under any circumstance. If you do so, there is a chance that attackers could use this information to steal all of your cryptocurrency funds.

5 / ALT COINS – PROS AND CONS

WHAT ARE ALT COINS?

ALT COINS, the most popular of which is Bitcoin, is a digital currency that enables instant payments to anyone, anywhere in the world. It can be converted into "real" money and traded for goods or services. Though it doesn't exist physically like other currencies (think paper bills), it can be accepted as if it were legal tender when a person trades goods or services.

A BRIEF HISTORY

E-gold began issuing a digital currency in 1996 that was accepted like traditional gold except it was stored on electronic cards rather than in coins or vaults. E-gold became popular because people could convert their wealth into gold and move them around easily with an ATM card just as they would with a traditional checking account.

The Birth of Bitcoin

In 2008, Satoshi Nakamoto released a white paper outlining the Bitcoin concept that was published on an obscure cryptography mailing list. Soon, it was being traded on a few underground forums. As time went by, more online communities began to accept Bitcoins as payment for goods and services. It wasn't until early 2013 that Bitcoins began to float higher in value.

It grew from less than $20 to $200 in just a few months before dropping back down again. In April of 2013, one Bitcoin was worth around $140 USD then saw a huge spike, reaching upwards of $266 USD in late November 2013 before dropping back down to around $180 USD.

The media covered the rise and fall of the Bitcoin, mostly because the value was so incredibly volatile. This was great for business because it had all the makings of an action-packed Hollywood movie.

For example, in April 2013, Bitcoin miner James Howells from Wales in the United Kingdom threw away a hard drive containing 7,500 Bitcoins worth $300m million at today's prices believing that he had transferred the bitcoin wallet to a new computer. Can you imagine?! In November of 2013, an individual in Jacksonville Florida purchased two Papa John's pizzas for 10,000 Bitcoins. That might seem like a lot of money now but it was worth less than enough for two pizzas at the time. In fact back then bitcoins did not have a value attached to them and the novel idea of trading digital currency for pizza was incredibly cool to Laszlo Hanyecz.

The media also likes to thank the creator of Bitcoin, Satoshi Nakamoto. This unknown individual released the master plans for Bitcoin on January 9, 2009 but disappeared shortly thereafter. Some suspect that he is actually former NSA employee and cryptographic expert, Nick Szabo.

PROS OF ALT COINS:

1. Alt coins are more secure than traditional money.

Alt coins are more secure because their minting is based on cryptography algorithms that are harder to hack. For example, the Bitcoin protocol uses encryption and a series of distributed network nodes to check all transactions to determine whether there are any discrepancies. This is what makes each transaction unique from the preceding one.

2. Alt coins are decentralized

They aren't physically printed in a central bank and then distributed via banks or any other financial institution. They exist only in cyberspace as a digital currency that can be sent directly between users without relying on any third parties such as banks or government organizations.

3. Alt coins can be used anywhere in the world, 24/7.

According to a recent IBM study, over 2.5 billion people are now connected to the internet. Alt coins can be exchanged for real money via online digital currency exchanges and used to purchase goods and services on the internet.

4. Alt coins are fast

They can be sent anywhere in the world without having to rely on slow third-party organizations such as banks or other financial institutions that charge fees for their services. These transactions occur directly between users using cryptographic technology, so they can be completed within minutes rather than days or weeks.

5. Alt coins promote innovation

These new forms of digital money encourage new types of services and businesses that would otherwise not exist due to high transaction fees associated with traditional online payment methods such as PayPal or credit cards.

6. Alt coins increase the efficiency of transactions

Banks can charge anywhere from 1-4% to process currency transactions. Online exchanges also charge a fee for their services, so it is best to use these instead, even though the fee is small relative to other charges imposed by third-party organizations.

7. Alt coins are deflationary

One of the main problems facing traditional money today is inflationary pressures due to an excessive amount of currency in circulation. With Bitcoin, only 21 million Bitcoins will ever be created, making them a scarce commodity, like gold and silver.

8. Alt coin transactions are recorded publicly and are easily blockchain verifiable.

Every transaction that has ever occurred since the first Bitcoin was created in 2009 can be traced back to its origin on the blockchain. The blockchain is a public ledger that records transactions chronologically and publicly so anyone can see which entities own whatever number of Bitcoins at any time.

9. Alt coins are relatively easy to acquire.

Bitcoins can be purchased in small fractions from online

digital currency exchanges, which means you don't have to spend $100 USD on Bitcoins all at once.

10. Alt coins can be used to protect your identity.

Due to the decentralized nature of alt coins, they don't have a central database that can be hacked or stolen from electronically, nor are they subject to identity fraud.

11. Alt coins can be backed up and encrypted so you don't have to worry about physically losing them or having them stolen from you.

There are many different encryption software packages that you can download and use on your computer that will enable you to encrypt your wallet and back it up so no one else can access your Bitcoins. If someone does somehow manage to hack into your system, the intruder would not be able to spend those Bitcoins without knowing your private key for each address in which those Bitcoins reside.

12. You can trade a wide range of goods and services with alt coins instead of just a limited number of products or services like regular money does; you are therefore unlikely to experience a deflationary spiral. Alt coins can be used to purchase virtually anything that can be bought online. This is important because unskilled labor and services are valued at their cost of production rather than what they can be sold for on the market. Therefore, if you have unskilled labor or services that you wish to exchange for alt coins, you can do this without worrying about what the outcome will be in terms of inflationary pressures.

13. Alt coins are more durable than regular money

They exist only as long as there is a community around them

supporting and using them, which means they aren't likely to disappear overnight due to political reasons or any other factor outside of the control of alt coin users and developers.

CONS OF ALT COINS:

1. Alt coins are not legal tender in any country, and therefore, you can never be 100% sure that you will be able to convert your alt coin assets back into regular money. Bitcoin has no set value in terms of regular money, which means that the average user will have to use some sort of exchange rate or a converter when converting between the two for comparison purposes.

2. Alt coins are subject to extreme price volatility and therefore represent a much riskier investment vehicle than regular money.

3. There is no insurance protecting your investment, so if the company goes out of business, there's nothing you can do about it, and your money will be gone forever.

4. If you have to liquidate your alt coin assets, the process of transferring them to a regular money-equivalent will be inherently complicated and time-consuming.

5. Many of the smaller alt coin communities are not very welcoming to newcomers in terms of getting people started with setting up a wallet and obtaining the coins. There is often a lot of emphasis on mining or faucets that drain your resources rather than helping you out.

6. Because alt coins are not legal tender in any country, you run the risk of having your crypto-assets frozen by a

government that is suspicious of cryptocurrencies or simply just wants to take action against them for whatever reason.

7. Alt coins have been around less time than Bitcoin has and therefore there is no reliable track record indicating how long they can be expected to survive.

8. Alt coins are generally not as stable as regular money, which means that they could be more susceptible to the effects of inflation over the long-term if their price continues to rise exponentially. This is particularly problematic if you are trying to save for a specific purpose such as buying a house or a car down the road, etc.

6 / HOW TO TRADE CRYPTOCURRENCY, A STEP-BY-STEP BLUEPRINT

TO TRADE CRYPTOCURRENCY, you should follow the steps below:

STEP 1: FIND A BITCOIN EXCHANGE THAT SUITS YOUR NEEDS

So, how do you do this? You need to know the cryptocurrency you want to trade and the type of exchange it is available on.

STEP 2: REGISTER FOR AN ACCOUNT WITH YOUR CHOSEN BITCOIN EXCHANGE

Some exchanges may require ID verification and other personal information before you can sign up. However, this process varies depending on the site, so be sure to read their guidelines if you are unsure what is required.

STEP 3: VERIFY YOUR ACCOUNT

In verifying your account, the exchange will hold your funds in a temporary "holding tank" until they are verified. This is done for your account's security. Most exchanges will only hold these funds for a few days at most, but up to one week is not uncommon.

STEP 4: DEPOSIT CURRENCY INTO YOUR ACCOUNT VIA BANK TRANSFER OR CREDIT CARD

While many exchanges accept PayPal, the fees associated with this payment method make it less desirable due to the amount of time required for processing. Bank transfers are best if you want fast and reliable trading features on your site because they do not carry any additional costs and are usually very quick.

Some exchanges will allow you to purchase crypto assets using credit or debit cards, but not all of them provide this service. If this is an important factor for you, make sure that your selected exchange provides this option before finalizing any trades with them.

STEP 5: BUY BITCOIN

Once you have deposited funds into your account, just navigate to the "Buy/Sell" page and select the amount of Bitcoin you would like to purchase.

STEP 6: TRANSFER BITCOIN TO YOUR OWN WALLET

Once you have purchased your first coin, it's best practice to immediately transfer it off of the exchange platform onto a wallet that you control. This will make sure that there is no possibility of an exchange hack or other compromise interfering with your funds in the future. It will also help protect your investment should the exchange become unattended or otherwise be offline for any reason.

STEP 7: TRADE BITCOIN FOR OTHER CRYPTOCURRENCIES, AND VICE VERSA

This is the fun part. Once you have Bitcoin in a secure location, you can buy other cryptocurrencies by trading in Bitcoin on a cryptocurrency exchange. Just like traditional stock exchanges, cryptocurrency exchanges allow you to place buy and sell orders to trade currencies based on their value relative to one another.

The price of each coin will change depending on the market and demand for it in the future, so it's always important to know how much your cryptocurrency is worth at any given time.

STEP 8: TRANSFER YOUR CURRENCY BACK OFF THE EXCHANGE

The final step is to send your currency to a wallet that you own (or just keep it in the exchange if that's where you plan to keep trading from).

Always remember, in trading cryptocurrency, you are investing in the future value of whatever coin you're buying, so always be careful that you aren't overspending on your purchase.

The best way to avoid this is to ensure that your budget allows you to take a healthy profit on your investment. If the price of the cryptocurrency actually goes up after you buy it, even better! Just be sure not to purchase more than what you can afford to lose, and you should be able to see some great returns without any trouble whatsoever.

7 / FACTORS THAT DETERMINE IF CRYPTO WILL MAKE YOU MONEY OR LOSE YOU MONEY

When dealing with cryptocurrency there are times that you will make money, and sadly, there are times that you will lose money. Now the question is, how do you know if your investment will make you money or lose it? Join us for a quick breakdown of some of the factors that determine if cryptocurrency will make you money or lose it.

There are numerous aspects that go into deciding whether or not an investment will generate gains, such as the market fluctuation in price of a coin and the amount of effort taken to research said coin; however, there are factors that stand apart from all others and they are as follows:

THE AMOUNT OF DETERMINATION YOU PUT INTO STUDYING A COIN

The amount of understanding you have for a coin determines if cryptocurrency makes you money or lose it. If you don't understand the coin, then chances are that your investment will make you lose money because you're not well-versed in what is going on, and so you'll be making uninformed decisions. However, if you do understand the coins' workings, then the majority of your investments will be well-informed, strong cryptocurrencies with bright futures, and so they will come back to the plus side of your balance sheet.

The amount of effort you put into researching a coin will determine if it will make or lose you money.

THE EXPANSE OF EFFORT YOU PUT INTO HOLDING A COIN

The amount of effort you put into *holding* a coin will determine you will gain money or lose it by trading in the currency.

Like with the amount of effort you put into researching a coin, if you're not willing to hold a coin for an extended period of time, then chances are that your investment will leave you with less money in your pocket. However, if you are willing to hold a coin throughout its ups and downs, then the money in your pocket will grow on the aggregate scale.

THE TIMING OF YOUR INVESTMENT

The timing of your investment can also affect your gains. With timing, you have two options. Either buy a coin early and sell it late, or buy a coin late and sell it early.

By buying a coin early in its inception and selling it later at a time when it has become prolific and adopted, you will end up with a higher value for the same number of coins because the value of the coin increases over time as either more are exchanged for money or mined. However, if you buy a coin late in its inception, i.e. after it peaked in investment and then sell it soon after buying it, then chances are that you will lose money. This is where being trading savvy and attitude to risk come into play.

YOUR COMFORT WITH RISK

Risk is the term generally used to describe the probability of a negative event in your trading activities. In other words an event which goes the other way of what you intended. With any trading the risk of such occurrences are very real and these translate to making losses.

When trading in cryptocurrencies, one is exposed to five types of financial risks:

- **Credit Risk** is the probability of parties involved failing to fulfil obligations and is mostly the result of theft and fraud. For example, in 2018 Binance was hacked and $40 million were lost as a result.
- **Legal Risk** is the probability of a negative event with regulatory rules which could be in the form of a ban on cryptocurrency trading in a given country as in fact happened when the states of Texas and North Carolina issued cease-and-desist orders to the Bitconnect crypto exchange due to suspicion of fraud.
- **Liquidity Risk** refers to the chance of the inability

to convert one's given trading position to fiat currencies. This risk is lessened by one's ability to make direct purchases using a cryptocurrency.
- **Market Risk** is caused by coin price fluctuations contrary to your expectation.
- **Operational Risk** is caused by the inability to trade, deposit, or withdraw into a crypto wallet.

Your comfort with any of the above risks will determine how your cryptocurrency trading project performs, whether it makes or loses you money. If you're not comfortable with risk, then chances are that your investment will cause you to lose money because when the value of a coin drops, you will likely join most investors in selling off your digital assets.

However, if you are comfortable with risk, then the majority of your investments will be worth more money as time goes by, and so they will increase your own gains.

In terms of risky investment, willingness to take risks on new investments can be broken down into two parts: willingness to take big risks and willingness to take little risks.

If you are not willing to take big risks, then chances are that your investment will make you lose money because you will only invest in coins that aren't risky and so won't produce any big gains. However, if you're willing to take big risks, you have a chance to hit on the "next big thing." The caveat to that is that riskier crypto investments are, by definition, riskier, meaning that they fail more often or do not have the same stability of more traditional currency investments.

THE COIN'S POTENTIAL

Potential can be broken down into three categories: high potential, medium potential and low potential.

- **High potential** coins are a risky investment but have the most potential to pay-off big time in the long run. They will have a lot of ups and downs within their time frame, which varies from one hour or one day to a year, but if you know how to ride the waves, then they will produce a lot of profit for you.
- **Medium potential** coins are a bit more stable than high potential coins but won't have as much upswing in price as high potential coins.
- **Low potential** coins aren't likely to produce any substantial gains unless the rest of the market has an extraordinary shift upward.

THE AMOUNT OF THE COIN'S DEVELOPMENT

The amount of technological development and rules a cryptocurrency has will determine if it makes you money or loses it. If the coin has a lot of development within its time frame then it will produce great amounts of gains, but if development is lacking then the majority of its potential will be limited.

THE COIN'S VOLUME

The amount of volume a cryptocurrency has will determine if it makes or loses you money. If the coin has a lot of volume within a period of time, then it will produce greater amounts of gains because people will be trading the coin more often, and so they'll be generating more capital for you by raising and lowering the price.

YOUR TIMEFRAME

The quantity of time that you devote looking at your investment will determine if it makes you money or loses it. If you only look at your investments once a month, then it is very likely that the value of your investment will change dramatically, and it'll be hard to make any money. Nevertheless, if you are eager to spend a lot of time looking at the value changes, then you'll be able to tell when the coin will get up and when it will drop so you can sell off before the price drops and buy high before the price gets up. If you want to make money it is best to set and forget it for a number of years. This way you are leaving it to miners to bring more into circulation and others to trade in the short term with more risk to you. For example bitcoin was worth the equivalent of eight cents when it started. It rose to $15.25 in August 2012 only to fall to $10.50 in a matter of minutes later. Today, in March 2021 each Bitcoin is valued to be the equivalent of $50,800.20. So if you bought $200 worth of bitcoin in 2009 when bitcoin started, you would have amassed there and then 2,500 bitcoins. If you then left that in your wallet and had a look twelve years later in March 2021, you would have earned to value of $127,000,500.00 with the same amount of coins. Also consider that this is low risk you. If it all went pear shaped then you would have lost $200, not the end of the world right? You did not need to actively trade or mine for which investment in hardware and recurring expenses in electricity bills are incurred.

8 / THE MOST EFFECTIVE, PROVEN,
AND TESTED WAYS TO INCREASE
YOUR SUCCESS RATE BY 10X
WHEN INVESTING IN
CRYPTOCURRENCY

INVESTING in Cryptocurrency can be an exhilarating and at the same time terrifying experience. There are a ton of things to consider, from whether you should invest in Bitcoin or Ethereum to how you store your cryptocurrency assets. However, there are ways that you can improve your success rate by 10x when investing in cryptocurrency.

FIRST, **understand the basics.**

When you first start investing, it is very important to understand what cryptocurrency is. Cryptocurrency is a form of digital money that is used and exchanged digitally. It is not issued or controlled by a central authority. Cryptocurrency uses cryptography to track transactions and generate currency units of account. This means that the transactions are secured using encryption methods. Cryptocurrency can be categorized as either a coin or a token (as in ICO).

. . .

NEXT, decide which platform you want to go with.
There are several platforms on which you can invest in cryptocurrencies. The best five are:

- Coinbase
- Binance
- Robinhood
- Gemini
- Kraken

As an investor, you are mostly concerned with the first 2 options, because they give you a higher likelihood of doing well and making more money. There is no better place for an investor to start than on the cryptocurrency trading platforms because usually they have great liquidity, transparency, good customer support, and a variety of coin listings.

Many investors who put their faith in ICOs have lost over 90% of their investment after listing on the exchange. There is a risk involved in all these types of investments. It is, however, important to always do your research well, particularly when it comes to ICOs.

CHOOSE the trading platform that is right for you.
There are some trading platforms that you can use to invest in cryptocurrencies. The choice of a trading platform will depend on the type of cryptocurrency investor you are. You can choose from:

- *Cryptocurrency exchanges:* These exchanges let individuals trade cryptocurrencies for other assets or coins. They may also allow investors to buy or sell cryptocurrency using fiat money (like USD).
- *Brokers:* Brokers offer a more extensive selection of altcoins, and they usually facilitate direct trades between buyers and sellers without the need for a third-party intermediary such as an exchange.

A good broker will make things much easier for you and give you a clear overview of how much you are making or losing.

Most Brokers do not facilitate buying Ripple yet as it is still an unknown cryptocurrency to most people. They also don't facilitate buying IOTA or NEO as they are only traded against other cryptocurrencies on small exchanges. Investing in altcoins is risky. However, the riskiest option is investing directly in Bitcoin due to its volatility and price fluctuation.

Investing in cryptocurrency involves perhaps a bit of risk, but if done right, it can make you a lot of money. Volatility plays an integral part in any crypto-investment and so do emotions. Remember that cryptocurrency was created to change the way we view money and investments as a whole. It will therefore take a bit of getting used to.

Do your research before investing in any cryptocurrency.

Don't just hop on the bandwagon and join the movement. Always have a reasonable backup plan in case your investment fails to produce the profits you anticipated.

Besides, don't just invest in one cryptocurrency; diversify your investments so that you can ride out drops in value in case one coin does not do well against another.

Finally, don't be afraid to experiment with different approaches because there is no such thing as a set formula for cryptocurrencies yet. There is still a lot of room for innovation in this space. However always be attentive to market forces of demand and supply to enable yourself to know what to do next. Remember this is not a gambling game of chance unless you want it to become one.

To improve your return on investment keep these ten tips constantly in mind:

1. **Have a motive for each trade** because purpose underpins you success. Crypto trading is a zero sum game meaning that someone wins and somebody else loses. Patience has to be the order of the day as cryptocurrencies are controlled by large account holders patiently waiting for total beginners to come in with guns blazing. Play the long game and be as invisible as possible.
2. **Set profit targets and use stop losses** – in other words know when to get out whether you are making profit or not. If for instance you acquired a coin at $500 er that as the minimum point at which you are willing to trade your coin. This will ensure that you always walk away with your initial investment. If you make a profit and leave this in the system then you will be trading with house money from that point onwards. However

using stop losses should not be abandoned even then.
3. **Overcome FOMO** which is short for *fear of missing out*. This mindset is the topmost reason why traders fail. Don't join a hunt when there is a feeding frenzy and the hype reaches news on TV. When such events materialize – sell or do nothing. When the event is over and the value drops, buy awaiting the next feeding frenzy event at which point you sell to make profit.
4. **Manage Risks** by staying put and gather small but regular and sure profits.
5. **Volatility depends on underlying assets** – altcoins depend on the current market value of Bitcoin. So when Bitcoin goes up, altcoins go down and of course the reverse is also true. So but altcoins when Bitcoin goes up and sell them when Bitcoin goes down.
6. **Low prices are not your reason to buy** – instead decide on which coin to invest in according to its market cap. The higher the coin's market cap the more it is suitable to invest in.
7. **Know the ICO catch** – true there are seemingly high returns investing during an Initial Coin Offering (ICO), however, a huge number of these have turned out to be scams through which millions have been lost. As with anything of this nature carry out background checks on the who is involved in the project, analyzing their ability to deliver what they promise and determine the

viability of the ICO idea by questioning everything in their white paper. If you are a novice – stay away!
8. **Do not hold Altcoins for too long** because they lose value in the long term. For long term holdings invest in Etherium (ETH), Factor (FCT), Monero (XRM) and Dash as these all have decent trading volumes. Whatever you do pay attention to price spikes on the charts and determine what the trend is.
9. **Diversify** by not investing your whole investment budget solely in cryptocurrencies.
10. **Use the goal setting feature by placing sell orders** by making sure you set revenue targets by placing sell orders in the order books. You can never tell when your asking price will be met to make your desired earnings. With sell orders you also encounter fewer transaction fees. Keep your cool and never accept offers for less than your asking price. Whatever you do train yourself to become decisive with getting in and out of trade.

9 / TOP 21 CRYPTOCURRENCY AROUND THE WORLD

HERE ARE the top 21 most prominent cryptocurrencies right now.

BITCOIN

Bitcoin is the "original" cryptocurrency (or one of them). Created in 2009, it has a number of advantages: low transaction costs; anonymity (although not total anonymity); independence from institutions like governments and banks; and decentralization which means that no single person or group can control it.

ETHEREUM

Ethereum is a cryptocurrency that offers additional features beyond those offered by Bitcoin. There are plans in the works to create a distributed autonomous corporation (i.e. a decentralized autonomous organization represented by computer encoded rules and governed by users not a central authority) using Ethereum as well as a way to exchange contracts using blockchains. A lot of major corporations have expressed interest in using Ethereum's services; for example, Toyota has agreed to work with the Ethereum team on developing self-driving cars.

LITECOIN

Litecoin is a fork of Bitcoin, created in 2011 by Charlie Lee (who would later go on to found Coinbase). It is similar to Bitcoin but easier to use for smaller payments and fast confirmations. It also has a faster block generation speed, which means that transactions are confirmed more quickly.

RIPPLE

Ripple is a cryptocurrency and payment network that targets banks and global payments rather than individuals. In addition to being able to send currency between two parties instantly (similar to PayPal or Venmo), it includes some features that would appeal to banks: instant confirmations, additional anonymity, and the ability for currency exchange.

IOTA

IOTA is an open-source cryptocurrency designed specifically for machines in the "Internet of Things" environment, a growing area of technology that involves connecting devices like cars, appliances, and more with networks in order to improve their functionality. Some of the uses include: electric car battery charging, smart appliances ("smart" fridges that can order groceries when supplies run low or connected washing machines that can alert you when a load is done), and self-driving cars.

NEM

NEM is an ambitious cryptocurrency platform that hopes to offer many services beyond simply being a currency. Its goal is to be "the new shiny Bitcoin." It offers a wide variety of features such as messaging, asset trading, encrypted messaging, voting systems, and more.

STELLAR LUMENS

Stellar Lumens is similar to Ripple but easier to use and free for institutions like banks and remittance companies. Stellar Lumens are currently used by IBM's blockchain services, Deloitte, and the National Bank of Abu Dhabi.

CARDANO

Cardano is a cryptocurrency designed specifically for use in developing nations and not just for individuals. Smart contracts are an essential portion of the Cardano system, enabling things like automatic bill paying and smart government benefits distribution. Its founder, Charles Hoskinson is also the co-founder of Ethereum.

EOS (ETHEREUM-ON-STEROIDS)

EOS is another cryptocurrency that aims to provide a solution to scalability issues facing Ethereum and other cryptocurrencies currently on the market. It offers more transactions per second and doesn't require as much RAM as Ethereum to run. Block.one, the team behind EOS, has already released a number of products; the most popular is a cloud storage provider called BitShares.

TRON

Tron is another ambitious cryptocurrency project aimed at the entertainment industry with features like decentralized storage and smart contracts for ticketing. It's led by famous Chinese entrepreneur Justin Sun who was formerly involved in Ripple Labs (and created Peiwo, an audio-based social media app with ten million users).

DASH

Dash is a cryptocurrency that bids "immediate" transactions, "private" transactions, and an optional decentralized governance system. The developers of Dash believe that these features make it ideal for smaller purchases (like those made at the grocery store).

NEO

NEO was started by Da Hongfei, a famous Chinese entrepreneur who founded a number of companies including OnChain, a startup focused on blockchain projects in China. NEO is similar to Ethereum but aims to do more for the Chinese government while staying out of China's regulatory jurisdiction.

MONERO

Monero is a newer cryptocurrency that improves on some of the privacy issues surrounding Bitcoin. It uses something called ring signatures to make transactions anonymous.

GOLEM

Golem is another cryptocurrency project focused on "global marketplaces" for buying and selling CPU power, which can be used for computations and data analysis or, in some cases, for running apps that need a lot of computing power (like video rendering or machine learning). The goal is to create "the first decentralized supercomputer."

TEZOS

Tezos is a cryptocurrency project with the main goal of creating a new governance model for cryptocurrencies (as opposed to relying on donations like Bitcoin Beeker). It's helmed by Arthur and Kathleen Breitman (husband and wife). It was embroiled in a scandal over the tech it was supposed to be based on, so it remains to be seen whether or not it successfully solves the governance problem.

OMISEGO

OmiseGO is focused on creating "the new financial system" through the use of cryptocurrencies, which they hope will disrupt the existing financial system in underdeveloped countries like Thailand or Vietnam.

DNOTES

DNotes is a digital currency that includes some extra features including a rewards program and a wiki for newcomers to learn about cryptocurrencies.

ZCASH

Zcash is similar to Monero but includes zk-SNARKs, making it a privacy protecting digital currency. It transacts efficiently and safely, with low fees while at the same time making sure digital transactions remain private. Most cryptocurrencies expose your full transaction history and holdings to everyone, buts Zcash transactions are completely private.

Similarly to Bitcoin, Zcash transaction data is posted to a public blockchain; but unlike Bitcoin, Zcash gives you the option of confidential transactions and financial privacy through shielded addresses. Zero-knowledge proofs allow transaction verification without revealing the sender, receiver or transaction amount. Selective disclosure features allow users the ability to share some transaction details, for purposes of compliance or audit.

NAVCOIN

Established in 2014 before the current wave of cryptocurrencies, NavCoin came about without any pre-mine or ICO, and has stood the test of time as well, continuing along at its own pace. It has seen features added since its inception, improvements made and upgrades to its codebase. This factor and its dedicated team ensure NavCoin continues to grow consistently.

NavCoin was built on the Bitcoin Core code, albeit with several changes. One such change was the addition of a subchain to the main blockchain which is called NavTech and it is what enables mixing and the anonymization of transactions on the NavCoin blockchain. Another change was to replace Bitcoin's proof of work algorithm with proof of stake. Compared with Bitcoin, NavCoin is a lot faster and cheaper.

DOGECOIN

Dogecoin was formed as a meme and is now the 26th largest cryptocurrency in the world by market cap (it's worth about $623 million). Legendary "shibe" Shibetoshi Nakamoto was part of the group that launched Dogecoin. It's a popular cryptocurrency, but it's not one for serious investors.

STELLAR

Stellar is a cryptocurrency that seeks to connect all payment systems (like PayPal, ACH, or wire transfers) and lets them use an international currency called Lumens for transactions. It aims to be a full transaction solution that can work with every existing payment method and currency around the world.

10 / FREQUENTLY ASKED QUESTIONS
ABOUT CRYPTOCURRENCY
INVESTMENT

THANKS TO BITCOIN, cryptocurrency has been popularized and is now on everybody's radar. It is not unusual for people to wonder how it works, how they can invest in cryptocurrencies, and why doing so might be a good idea.

The first thing you should understand is that investing in cryptocurrencies isn't "investing" as such; instead, cryptocurrencies are speculation assets, i.e. assets bought with the hope these will become more valuable in the near future, and there's very little regulation around what you invest in or who you buy from. So, let us deal with the most commonly asked questions about cryptocurrency.

Q: What is cryptocurrency?
A: Cryptocurrencies are a form of digital currencies based on the blockchain technology. They can be used to pay for transactions using the particular currency or converted into fiat money (government-backed currency, such as the

USD, EUR, etc.). The most popular cryptocurrencies are Bitcoin (BTC), Ethereum (ETH), and Litecoin (LTC).

Q: How do cryptocurrencies work?

A: All cryptocurrencies are based on blockchain technology. This means that information about transactions is not recorded in a central place. Instead, all transactions that have ever taken place are stored in immutable digital blocks that require cryptographic validation to be spent. When cryptocurrency is sent from one address to another, the transaction is validated by miners. Combining information from several transactions, they create a new digital block that contains both and a hash of all the preceding blocks. This new block is then added to the chain of existing blocks and thus becoming part of the blockchain.

Q: What are mining pools? Why do people mine cryptocurrencies?

A: Mining pools consist of a group of people who work together to mine cryptocurrencies. They share resources and profits (if any) in proportion to their contribution. There are two reasons why people mine cryptocurrencies: it's either to earn money or because they support the technology behind it.

The first reason is obvious—if you join a mining pool, you can receive a reward for the work that your hardware has done. Each cryptocurrency has a different method of rewarding miners and there's no way to know which will be the most profitable one when you start mining. Some cryptocurrencies are designed to have a specific block time and difficulty that changes over time, while others are not. This latter allows to mine them almost indefinitely as their block rewards will continue growing with the value of their coins.

A lot of people mine cryptocurrencies because they support blockchain technology and think it has great potential in the future. They want to support the growth of the industry and earn money in the process.

Q: How do you mine cryptocurrency?

A: You can choose to mine cryptocurrencies by yourself or you can join a mining pool if you don't have hardware that's capable of mining profitably. If you're looking to join a mining pool, make sure they have a stable reputation, as many pools have recent history of problems with hacking and stealing coins. You should also make sure that your pool has automatic payout configured so that coins will be sent to your wallet on a regular basis.

As far as mining cryptocurrency by yourself is concerned, you need to have a suitable hardware and enough technical knowledge of how the particular cryptocurrency works. Mining profitability depends on a number of factors—the most important one being the cost of electricity, as it determines how profitable it is to mine one currency in comparison with other ones.

There are several websites that show you how much money you can earn by mining different cryptocurrencies.

They also show which ones are the most profitable now and in the future.

Q: How do you invest in cryptocurrencies?

A: Cryptocurrencies can be bought using fiat money (government-backed currencies such as the USD, EUR, etc.) or other cryptocurrencies. The first option is the most popular, and it's used by both beginners and experienced traders. When you buy cryptocurrency using fiat money, you're basically buying it from a cryptocurrency exchange, which accepts regular currency in exchange for cryptocurrency. These exchanges are designed to be as secure as possible because they store their clients' funds and need to comply with all applicable regulations regarding client identification, anti-money laundering and KYC (know your customer).

Q: What is the best cryptocurrency exchange?

A: The best cryptocurrency exchange depends on your needs. If you're looking for a place where you can make fiat currency deposits and withdrawals (bank transfers, credit card, or similar), then you'll want to go with a reputable exchange that accepts those payments. This includes Coinbase, CEX.io, Gemini, and Coinmama. If you want to trade for cryptocurrencies with other cryptocurrencies in an all-digital environment, then you might want to check out Binance or Poloniex.

. . .

Q: How to find reputable cryptocurrency exchanges?

A: Unlike fiat money, which is regulated by governments and banks, cryptocurrencies don't fall under the regulations of these conventional financial institutions. However, they still have to abide by rules and regulations that have been set up by the crypto industry. This can be seen in the form of self-regulations that have been adopted by most major cryptocurrencies such as Bitcoin, Ethereum, Ripple, and Litecoin. The majority of people who trade cryptocurrencies use regulated exchanges because it means their coins are always safe from theft or hacking.

Q: Are cryptocurrency investments safe?

A: The security of cryptocurrencies depends on the method you choose to store them. It's best to use cold storage such as a hardware wallet as much as possible because you can keep coins there that you aren't currently trading. Hardware wallets are much more secure than online/hot wallets which can be compromised remotely. If you keep your coins on an exchange, make sure to enable two-factor authentication, set up a strong password, and always check for regular updates. Other ways to secure cryptocurrency include using a hardware wallet (which is not connected to a computer) or using a paper wallet.

Q: When is the best time to buy cryptocurrencies?

A: It depends on your goals and expectations. If you believe in a cryptocurrency and see a good potential for it to grow in value, then there's probably no better time to buy than now. However, if you're planning on using cryptocurrencies for everyday transactions, it's probably not a good idea to invest heavily into them yet because they aren't widely accepted at the moment. The general rule of thumb is that you should only invest the money you can afford to lose because cryptocurrency prices fluctuate quite frequently.

Q: Why are cryptocurrencies so volatile?

A: Cryptocurrencies fluctuate because of the same reason why fiat money fluctuates - supply and demand. When demand for a cryptocurrency increases, its price will also increase. On the other hand, when the amount of that cryptocurrency in circulation decreases (due to coins being lost or stolen), then its price begins to decrease.

Q: Why is there an exponential rise in cryptocurrency prices?

A: The main reason why cryptocurrencies have risen exponentially over the past few years is because more and more people are beginning to see their true potential and recognize their huge benefits over fiat money such as national currencies. With the growing popularity of cryptocurrencies, more and more businesses are beginning to accept them as a form of payment.

Q: WHAT IS MEANT BY "HODL?"

A: In cryptocurrency terminology, HODL is an acronym for "Hold on for Dear Life." It refers to holding on to coins rather than selling them or trading them. It was first coined in 2013 by a cryptocurrency trader who was trying to encourage people not to panic at the time because the price of Bitcoin dropped by 21 percent over a period of just one week. The trader said that people should hold on and that it would be great if they could HODL during this difficult time. If people had listened to his advice, they would have more than tripled their gains since Bitcoin reached a high of $19,097.21 on December 17, 2017.

Q: What is the benefit of cryptocurrencies over paper money?

A: Cryptocurrencies are better than paper money in many ways such as transaction speed and simplicity.

- Transaction Speed: When an individual sends fiat currency over to another person or a business via the banking system, it may take several days for that person or business to actually receive and spend the money being sent. But when sending via a cryptocurrency, the transaction can be completed in as little as minutes.

Cryptocurrencies are also popular with the younger generation who have grown up with digital technology. They prefer to get their currency and spend it without delay.

- Simplicity: When you want to send money, all you need do is go to your wallet or your bank account and click the send button before you enter the recipient's address and how much you wish to send. The recipient will then similarly have to open their wallet or bank account and click on the 'receive' button before sending an address to which you can send this money.

Q: What are the benefits of cryptocurrencies over gold?
A: Cryptocurrencies like Bitcoin and Litecoin have many advantages over gold. Gold is a precious metal that offers a store of value as it can be exchanged for other items or services. However, it's not easy to send gold to someone else, as you must deal with delivery companies and banks. Furthermore, when you buy gold, you take on the physical risk that comes with storing it in your home or elsewhere.

Regarding ease of use, cryptocurrencies are far superior to gold. When you want to send gold to someone, you must physically transport it to them, and that can be hard to do in some cases. You also need to see that your gold is well protected at all times. Cryptocurrencies, on the other hand, allow for traders to easily transfer money around the globe within minutes.

Q: How do people acquire cryptocurrencies?
A: There are several ways people acquire cryptocurrencies. The first way is through mining. It also used for the cryptocurrency networks that allow new coins into their market. This happens in a process known as "mining" where the computers are used by cryptocurrency enthusiasts who solve complex mathematical equations. Miners verify the ledger of transactions to ensure it's all correct. In exchange

for solving these mathematical problems, the miners receive a small amount of cryptocurrency in the form of a reward. A second way to get cryptocurrencies is by buying them from an exchange that deals with cryptocurrencies and has a market value based on the current market prices. This is basically how people acquire any stock or currency. Finally, people can sell products or services in exchange for cryptocurrencies. There are different forms of this such as accepting cryptocurrencies directly or offering some sort of discount if customers pay using them.

11 / DIGITAL WALLETS FOR CRYPTOCURRENCY

CRYPTOCURRENCY IS an exciting and emerging technology that has a lot of potential to radically disrupt the world of economics as we distinguish it. However, figuring out how to actually use cryptocurrency can be really difficult. In order for crypto to become a mainstream payment option, people need access to wallets that are easy-to-use and secure. Here, we'll take you through the basics of digital wallets so you can start trading digital currency like Bitcoin with confidence.

WALLETS IN CRYPTOCURRENCY

Cryptocurrency wallets are essential for storing and managing your digital currency. You can think of digital wallets as being like a bank account. They allow you to send and receive Bitcoin or other cryptocurrencies like Ethereum, Dash, Zcash, etc. The main difference between traditional bank accounts and cryptocurrency wallets is that digital currency wallets aren't really stored by any single entity like a bank or government agency is. Instead, they are stored on computers all over the world, which means there is no one in control of them.

There is really no correct or incorrect way to use your cryptocurrency wallet.

TYPES OF WALLETS:

- Cold Wallets

Cold wallets refer to any digital wallet that is not connected to the internet. This includes flash drives, external hard drives, and even physical pieces of paper with your private keys written on them. As we have already seen only the owner of the private key can encrypt data. Conversely, while everyone can encrypt data with the public key only the owner of decrypt it. Therefore, anyone can send data securely to the private key owner. This is why private key safety is so important. Cold wallets are best for long-term storage of funds and are often used by people who want to buy large amounts of cryptocurrency and then hold for a long period of time.

- Hot Wallets

Hot wallets refer to any wallets that have an internet connection. These offer some great convenience because they are easy to use, but you do lose some privacy by allowing a third-party access to your funds via the web. Most exchanges offer online digital wallets as well as apps that you can use on your smartphone.

- Paper Wallets

A paper wallet refers to a physical piece of paper which has your public and private keys printed on it. Paper wallets are the most secure option for storing cryptocurrency because they do not require access to the internet but are also very difficult to use and maintain. Most people will never use a paper wallet, but they are an important tool for long-term investors, so make sure you understand them before purchasing large amounts of cryptocurrency.

- Brain Wallet

A brain wallet is a password-generated key that you memorize, rather than write down or save. These are an interesting new development that offers some additional security in exchange for added complexity. If you are watching for a more protected way of accessing your funds, this might be a good option, but always make sure that no one else knows your password!

- Soft Wallet

A soft wallet refers to a software program that can exist on your desktop or on your smartphone. These programs allow you to manage and access your cryptocurrency without ever having to directly access your private keys. They are very convenient but are not as secure as many cold storage options like hardware wallets.

Soft wallets offer some great convenience, and they make it easier for people to get started with cryptocurrency. If you are looking for a rapid method to start trading digital money, this might be the right option for you.

- Hardware Wallet

A hardware wallet is a definite physical device that is designed specifically for storing digital currency. They are very secure and can be accessed with a PIN or by physically connecting the device to your desktop computer. Hardware wallets are the most secure options available for storing cryptocurrency, but they do require some upfront investment in the form of a small digital device that plugs into your computer.

- Deterministic Wallets

A deterministic wallet refers to a wallet that will generate a new private key every time you want to receive funds. This will also create new addresses for you, so it is important to keep track of them. Deterministic wallets are an excellent option for people who are interested in developing applications that need specific addresses, but they can be confusing and frustrating for users who simply want to make payments or trade their cryptocurrency.

- Multisig Wallets

Multisig refers to any wallet with multi-signature security features. These are a great inkling for the reason that they let multiple parties to agree on how funds should be spent. This means that you can have a wallet with two out of three signatures required to spend your funds for added security. This is an excellent way to remove the single point of failure that is often associated with cryptocurrencies.

Multisig wallets are great from a technical perspective, but they can be frustrating for normal users who simply want to make purchases or cash out their cryptocurrency holdings. These wallets are best for advanced users and applications that require additional security measures.

- Vault

A vault refers to any multisig wallet that has additional features designed for advanced users with large holdings of crypto assets. These include built-in auditing and other anti-fraud features designed to prevent theft and loss from internal sources within the company running the vault.

WHAT ARE DIGITAL WALLETS?

A digital wallet is a software program that keeps your public and private keys for your digital currency. Your private key is used to unlock your wallet and is also how you sign off on transactions made from your account. The public key functions as a kind of an identifier that allows you to "communicate" with the network where your currency resides.

Digital wallets store all of the data about your balance, transactions, and more securely than you would be able to do yourself, making them an incredibly useful tool for investors who are serious about trading cryptocurrency.

IMPORTANCE OF KEEPING PRIVATE KEYS SAFE

It is important to treat the private keys for your digital wallets like cash; they are essentially the most valuable thing you have. If someone were to steal your private keys or hack into your account, they could use those keys to send all of your funds directly to their own digital wallet. Use strong passwords and never give access to your private keys to anyone.

DIGITAL WALLET PROVIDERS

There are several different kinds of digital wallets. Each one serves a different purpose, and some wallets can be used across multiple platforms. Here are the main ones to know:

- Coinbase — This is the most common type of digital wallet for beginners. It is an easy-to-use platform that allows you to buy and sell crypto through your bank account, credit card or PayPal account and once you make a purchase, you can store that currency in a Coinbase wallet.
- Cryptocompare — This is another beginner's tool

with easy-to-follow charts and simple information about the price history of various currencies. You cannot store currency on this website but it does provide valuable information on how currencies behave when they reach certain volumes.

- Cryptocurrency Exchange — This is for more advanced users who are looking to buy and sell cryptocurrency directly from exchanges rather than purchasing it from an individual. Exchanges have low transaction fees and often better prices for buying in bulk. However, they are not always so great for newbies since they tend to have complex interfaces that require technical knowledge of how the system works.
- Device management — This is another option for storing your cryptocurrency. Similar to digital wallets, device management works through the use of software that you download to your desktop or mobile device. It uses two-factor authentication and stores your private keys on your computer so that they are not accessible by any other parties.

Cryptocurrency wallets are an important tool if you want to be able to make transactions with cryptocurrency in a safe and secure manner.

MULTIPLE DIGITAL WALLETS

In addition to the various types of wallets, there are actually several different types of digital wallets that allow you access from a number of different devices. Think about how many times you may access your bank account on a daily basis; if you only had one bank account, it would be incredibly inconvenient and possibly not possible at all. In the future, many people predict that you will be able to have several different digital wallets that all operate under a single account or even within a single platform.

Digital currencies are growing more and more popular every day and this is only the beginning. With continued growth, it is likely that there will be hundreds of different types of wallets available, each with their own unique features. This is where the real potential for cryptocurrency lies; it has the potential to completely revolutionize how money operates in our society. If people can seamlessly move in and out of their cryptocurrency at any time, we might start to see a virtual currency as our primary form of payment rather than fiat currency.

12 / PROOF OF WORK (POW) AND PROOF OF STAKE (POS) IN CRYPTOCURRENCY

PoW AND PoS are two different methods of how a blockchain can be secure. Proof of Work requires that computers compute for blocks added to the cryptocurrency blockchain, thus completing missing chains for which a reward is received. Proof of Stake means that the more coins you have, the more chance you have at receiving rewards for solving puzzles and blocks. Let us dwell on these two more.

PROOF OF WORK (POW)

Proof of Work requires that miner(s) solve a computing problem in order to receive a reward. This is the reason why they are called "miners," and it refers to the fact that they must work hard to receive rewards.

Bitcoin uses PoW as means of securing its blockchain. All computers in the Bitcoin network are working extremely hard in order to answer the "hash puzzle," which is solved by finding an input that, when hashed, is smaller than a certain number. This number is a variable called difficulty, which changes every 2016 blocks (after this number of blocks all miners obtain their reward).

In case of Bitcoin, the first miner to find the solution receives 12.5 BTC plus all the fees the transactions in that block had. In some cases, it might also include a transaction with no fee, called "coinbase transaction." Each miner's computer that finds an answer also races against other miners to propagate their block faster in order to get the reward before someone else does. Therefore, Bitcoin has created what is known as a distributed consensus mechanism: it allows miners to agree on which are the valid blocks and order them chronologically. For a block to be valid it must hash to a value less than the current target meaning that each block indicates that work has been done generating it.

PROOF OF STAKE (POS)

Proof of Stake is a controversial approach because it is vulnerable to a so called "nothing at stake" attack. To be honest, I think about it as an attack but developers say that it's only theoretical. PoS requires that whoever holds coins has the ability to mine blocks and therefore receive rewards. If you look at the total supply of Bitcoins, you will find people with a huge amount of them. Therefore, they should have more chance at mining greater rewards just because they have more coins. However, this does not seem fair for smaller miners who also work hard on solving puzzles in order to receive their rewards.

In case of Proof of Stake, there is no mining involved. This is a consensus algorithm for blockchain based on randomly selected validators staking native network tokens by locking them into the blockchain, to produce and approve blocks. Every period (for example every time a minute, an hour or a day) the network selects one node from the pool (nodes are computers that are connected to the blockchain). The node goes to sleep for one second and once it wakes up it requires that all wallets signal it with a vote. If 51% of the wallets that have coins in them signal their approval, then this node will receive 100% of the reward instead of splitting it with other miners as in PoW.

The identification process between nodes and their owner/wallet is based on cryptography. It is a one-way process and so there is no traceable connection between the wallet and the node. In order to make it more secure, nodes with the same ID can only wake up after they have signal their approval together (it won't be one after another). In case of Bitcoin, this algorithm is called Proof of Stake Velocity (PoSV).

So, if you hold more coins in your wallet for a longer period of time, then you will also have a higher chance at earning block rewards. This might seem fair but there are other concerns as well. For example, people could run different wallets on the same computer in order to get more chances at receiving rewards. Also, there is a risk of centralization of a PoS system where the node that receives more votes will have more chances at receiving rewards. That's why some cryptocurrencies (for example Vertcoin) implemented the "cold staking" protocol in order to avoid this centralization.

PROS OF POW AND POS:

Large hash rate (number of computers mining at the same time) is required in order to have a secure blockchain. Blockchains that are based on PoW and PoS can achieve this because of the "stake" that miners have in them. If you hold more money/coins, you will be more incentivized to keep the blockchain secure so that you receive your rewards regularly. Developers say that PoW is more decentralized than PoS but this could be also debated as we look further into it.

PoS can be better for the environment because it does not require powerful computers to solve puzzles or mine new blocks.

THE CONS OF POW AND POS

They both require a lot of energy in order to function. This is not only the electricity that is wasted on mining but also the hardware that is needed to mine with. How much does crypto mining really consume?

In case of PoW, blocks are large and take more time in order to be mined. Therefore, they need to be smaller in size so that they could also take less time when being mined (for example 2 minutes instead of 10 minutes). This might cause a situation where more transactions are needed to be included into the blockchain in order for it to become bigger again.

In case of PoS, nodes can become more centralized because it is easier to buy a lot of coins in order to have a higher chance at helping the blockchain grow. Also, there is a risk if one node gets 51% of the votes and decides to break the consensus mechanism.

In case of PoW, it is possible that there are nodes with a high hash rate but they are not securing the network at all. For example, they could be separate from the main blockchain and work on their own blockchain in order to receive their rewards. This way, the main blockchain would lose its security as it will be forked by this new crypto currency that is based on PoW.

13 / MINING IN CRYPTOCURRENCY

WHAT IS MINING?

MINING IS the process of adding records to a blockchain. The miner can either be an individual mining on their own or a mining pool that pools the resources of many people.

Mining is a difficult process because it takes an input of computational power and time, which is why miners are awarded with Bitcoin. This award, also known as the block reward, allows the miner to create new Bitcoins. The size of this award decreases as time goes on to ensure that no more than 21 million Bitcoins are in circulation by 2140.

WHAT IS MINING FOR?

Miners collect transaction fees and/or newly created coins for their work. These coins are just like any other, they have one-time value and provide monetary incentive for miners in the form of funding new projects, promoting new laws, etc.

PROCESS OF MINING

The easiest way to know if you are mining is to see if you have an address for your account on any site offering cryptocurrency.

Let's Start Mining!
The first thing you will need to do is set up an address for yourself. This can be done by setting up an account on a cryptocurrency exchange. They will provide you with one free of charge. My personal favorite is Poloniex as they have the most possibilities to trade your coins in a matter of minutes. There are many exchanges available, just do your research and find one that suits your needs. Another option is to set up a Blockchain account. The easiest way to do this is to follow the tutorials on their website. Most sites are going with using Blockchain as their primary wallet provider due to their advanced security measures and ease of access through their website or app. Once you have your address, then you will need to download the mining software. I prefer to use Minergate because they allow you to mine from home with no additional hardware outlay.

To set up your miner, go to the ' Getting Started ' tab in Minegate and click on the highlighted button.

This will launch a new window.

Now, all you need to do is fill in your username, enter a strong password, check the box if you are okay with it remembering it and then hit ' login '.

Simply hit ' Start Mining, ' and the program will start to work, register for an account and follow the login process

Then click on the 'Wallet' button. And make sure that the wallet address on the left is unique to you and is not already used by someone else.

You have now set up mining.

If at any time, if you need to close out of your miner just click on the 'Close' tab in the upper right corner. This will exit the program and save your progress so far.

WHY DO I SEE AN 'INVALID NONCE' ERROR?

Nonce refers to the random number that your miner uses when completing the block. The problem is not that you are not mining, it is that someone else is also mining with the same random number at the same time as you and has already completed a block. To solve this problem just click on the 'Reset Nonce' button.

This will launch a new window and start a new round of mining for you.

WHAT IS A POOL?

A pool is any group of miners working under the same goal, to mine more and generate more cryptocurrency for themselves. It allows you to mine the same cryptocurrency faster as you are combining the total hashing power of all of your workers. This also gives leverage against hardware failures as one piece of hardware malfunctioning does not affect the entire pool and potentially ruin it. On average there are two possible answers when mining a block using proof-of-work (PoW) methodology, one block will be validated by one miner and another by another miner. Whichever block gets validated first defines which answer will be picked.

TYPES OF MINING POOLS:

- Slush Pool: one of the first mining pools created; no registration required and payouts work on a PPS system (pay-per-share); 3% fee charged by pool operator.
- Antpool: Chinese mining pool, known to be the biggest mining pool of Bitcoin; payouts work on a PPLNS (pay-per-last-n-shares) system and charges a 2% fee.
- BTC.com: combines both solo and pooled mining; charges 1% fee and payouts work on a PPS system.

WHERE CAN I FIND A POOL?

The first and easiest place to look is their website. The second-best option is to go to getcrypto.info and look through the list of pools available there. Thirdly, if you want one that is up and running, then I recommend you use Minergate. Don't forget you can set it up for free on your computer and mine directly from there.

CRACKING THE CODE TO CRYPTOCURRENCY INVESTMENTS / 89

WHAT IS THE EASIEST POOL TO USE?

There is no easy answer for this. I tend to use Minergate because it is free, and they are always looking for new miners. They have a large user base, so it is harder to win mining rewards, but if you don't mind waiting or you are simply looking to get started, then this would be my recommendation. There are many other options that you can find by doing your own research, just be careful as some of them will attempt to steal your cryptocurrency/hardware or otherwise scam you out of it.

WHAT IS THE BEST MINING SOFTWARE?

This is a very subjective question, and there are many different answers. In addition to Minergate, there are other options out there, such as NiceHash. Here are some others:

- **Minergate** is my preferred option for mining because it is free and easy to use. However, you can only mine on it if you have a Windows PC.
- **NiceHash** is good because they have a large community and most of the pools available in their search are already running. This is useful if you want to start mining right away with the least amount of time setting up.
- **TeraPool** also has a large user base and they accept Bitcoin as payment as well as PayPal (as long as your PayPal email address starts with 'PayPal'). They provide a very powerful interface

that allows you to manage your workers across all of your different pools.

- **Empowercoin** is a powerful system that allows you to rent out your unused CPU power to anyone else in the system. This is a great option if you want to make some extra money while you aren't using your computer. You can choose how much power you rent out and how much power you use, and then it will match up sellers with buyers in the system based on how much they are willing to pay for various levels of usage.
- **Bitcoin Hivemind** isn't really a mining program, but it is useful because it integrates directly into your wallet so that you can see which blocks are getting mined by which miners as well as other stats as they come online. It is most useful for people who mine on the Bitcoin network, but you can also look at other currencies.

HOW CAN I OPTIMIZE MY MINING EXPERIENCE?

There are many different ways to do this. You can set up autorun so that the system starts mining when you turn on your computer. You can also overclock your video card to get more performance out of it, but be aware this increases the power consumption and heat output.

14 / INITIAL COIN OFFERINGS
     (ICOS)

INITIAL COIN OFFERINGS (ICOs) are a new trend in funding cryptocurrencies and other projects. It is a way for creators of new and interesting projects to raise money, while investors can capitalize on the potential for growth in the developing industry that is cryptocurrency. This part will explore the idea of an ICO, provide some background information on this phenomenon, and offer advice to those who may be interested in buying into such an event.

HOW DOES ICOS WORKS?

The way ICOs function is that a creator of a new cryptocurrency will put out information in the form of a whitepaper or message board post. The creator will explain what the project is about, what should happen if it succeeds, and how the investors will be rewarded. The amount of tokens sold to investors and the investment cap are determined as well. Once all this information is determined, the creators release their coins to buyers for purchase, as long as no cap has been reached. Money raised from investors during an ICO goes directly toward funding the project in question.

HOW DO THEY RAISE MONEY?

ICOs raise money through blockchain technology crowd-funding platforms, which mainly exist on Ethereum's blockchain platform. Ethereum is one of the most prevalent platforms designed specifically for funding ICOs. The process for an ICO on Ethereum's platform is as follows:

1. The ICO creator creates a smart contract on Ethereum's blockchain. This smart contract contains all the information about the new token, including what it's worth, how many tokens will be created, and how investors will be rewarded if the project succeeds.
2. A cryptocurrency exchange is launched on Ethereum's platform that allows people to invest in the new ICO token by paying in Bitcoin or Ethereum. People can buy and sell tokens like stocks through this exchange after they are released by its creators.
3. The ICO creator releases the tokens to investors if the investment cap has not already been reached.
4. Investors who participated in the ICO may consider selling their newly purchased tokens at an exchange, which can be done by using the cryptocurrency exchange created for that purpose.

WHY SHOULD ONE INVEST IN AN ICO?

Potential investors should consider investing in an ICO because of these reasons:

- A new and potentially lucrative investment opportunity exists where people can buy into new projects before they take off and sell them at a profit once they succeed.
- ICOs raise money by creating new coins, which have their own blockchain on Ethereum's platform. These new coins may be tradeable on the cryptocurrency exchange created for the ICO, or after they are released to investors.
- ICOs allow people to invest in a project that they believe in before it comes out and profit from it once it does.

WHAT SHOULD ONE LOOK FOR?

Investors should look for these factors when deciding to participate in an ICO:

- Consider the potential of the project. If it's something that you believe will succeed, then it's worth investing into.
- Research the team behind the new ICO to ensure they have what it takes to see their project through. Look at their background, experience, and predictions of feasibility.

- Do your own study and talk to others who have experience with ICOs. Other investors in the cryptocurrency world may know more about specific projects that you don't or can provide a different perspective than what you have yourself.

HOW TO BUY ICOS

There are two ways one can obtain tokens from an ICO:

1. The project creators' cryptocurrency exchange, which is funded by other cryptocurrencies purchased with fiat currency.
2. The cryptocurrency exchange created for ICOs on Ethereum's platform.

CAN I USE FIAT CURRENCY?

One cannot buy ICOs directly with fiat currency. Instead, they must be purchased with a different cryptocurrency that the creators will fund. For example, once Bitcoin is obtained, it may be used to purchase ICO tokens on the creators' exchange.

15 / COMMON RED FLAGS YOU NEED TO AVOID WITH CRYPTOCURRENCY INVESTMENTS

IF YOU KEEP these in mind and follow our advice, you should be able to prevent some pretty painful losses that could otherwise happen.

Cryptocurrencies are still a very volatile asset class, and you should not invest money in any cryptocurrency that you cannot afford to lose. There is a good chance that cryptocurrency prices will plummet as quickly as they have risen. There is also a chance that they will skyrocket, but there is no way to know for sure which way the prices will move.

With all of that out of the way, let's go over some of the most common red flags that we see with cryptocurrency investments.

INFLATED TRADING VOLUME

The first thing that you need to do before even thinking about investing in a cryptocurrency is to look at the trading volume. You should be looking at the trading volume on more than one exchange. There are many examples of exchanges inflating their volume numbers by adding up the trades across different exchanges. The higher the trading volume, the more likely it is that there are a lot of people who are interested in buying and selling that cryptocurrency.

LONG EXCHANGE DELAYS

One of the biggest red flags for us when it comes to cryptocurrency trading is an exchange with very long order delays. The longer the order delay, the more time the exchange has to adjust your trade in their favor. So, you'll want to make sure that you're not getting in too late on a trade because someone else put an order in before you.

LOW TRADE VOLUME

The opposite of inflated trading volume is a low trading volume. If there is very little trading going on with your preferred cryptocurrency, then it may be due to lack of interest or lack of trader interest in that specific token.

LACK OF INFORMATION

You'll want to make sure that you're investing in a project that is transparent and that tells you what is happening in the community. It's normal for many projects to experience growth spurts as they get a lot of attention, but if there is no information being provided to the community, then it may be time to move on. If you can find out how frequently they post updates on social media then look for someone who posts regularly and answers questions from their followers.

LACK OF USE CASES

While looking at the project's social media to get an idea about their transparency, also look at their posts to get an idea of what they're doing with the technology. Someone may have created a new cryptocurrency, but is it actually being used in any way? Do they have a working product? If you can't find your answers by looking at their social media, then look at places like Reddit and Medium to see if you can find any helpful information.

UNREALISTIC GOALS

You should be looking at the project's goals and determining if they are realistic. A lot of people have unrealistic expectations for how much value their cryptocurrency will reach, but there is still plenty of room for growth if it is used as an actual currency instead. So, you'll want to look at their goals and see if they are within the realm of possibility.

ANONYMOUS DEVELOPERS: CREDIBILITY ISSUES

If the developers are anonymous, then you should be concerned about their credibility. It's really the job of the developers to sell this new token to investors, so it would make sense that they would want to be public about who is working on the project.

TEAM LACKS TECHNICAL EXPERIENCE

You should also be looking to see if the team has any sort of credibility or experience. A lot of people are putting a lot of money into these projects without doing much research, so you'll want to make sure that they are not just making their money from pumping and dumping. If there is no strategy for growing the community then it is likely that the project will fail before it even begins. You'll want to make sure that they have solid plans for how they will move forward with this project in the future.

LACK OF TRANSPARENCY

The most important thing when it comes to cryptocurrency investing is transparency. Without transparency, you will never be able to make a confident investment in any ICO, and this should be one of your first red flags. Look for information such as the whitepaper, the team members, their road map, and more. Make sure that you're getting all of this information before investing in any cryptocurrency.

Cryptocurrencies can be a great way to boost your portfolio if you handle them correctly. But keep in mind that there are many that are just flat-out scams. If you avoid these red flags then you should be able to maximize your profits from cryptocurrency trading.

16 / THE ROLE OF TECHNICAL ANALYSIS IN CRYPTOCURRENCY INVESTMENT

HERE WE WILL FOCUS on the role of technical analysis in cryptocurrency investment. We start by describing what is meant by technical analysis and then proceed to illustrate its relevance to cryptocurrency investment.

TECHNICAL ANALYSIS

Technical analysis is a study of changes in trends from prior knowledge, and it has been used as a technique for qualitative financial forecasting since the 1920s. It typically uses three core indicators: price movements, volume or trading activity, and moving averages. It can measure trends based on these physical variables, forecast future market behavior, deduce information about past prices by looking at their historical patterns, identify peaks or troughs within cyclical markets, indicate periods where market sentiment has shifted rapidly (i.e., identifying the start of a bubble), and determine when to buy or sell a security for substantial profits.

But what does this mean for cryptocurrency investment? In essence, it can be used as a tool to determine future movements in market prices. Determining price patterns that have formerly held true will assist you in your investment strategy and allow you to harness the collective experience of those who came before you. As long as one is aware of current trends, an understanding of how they might influence future price behavior can be invaluable.

The most common use of technical analysis is predicting where a market may go next based on its historical performance (trend analysis). This can be performed by comparing a given market to its historical prices. These comparisons are usually performed with the aid of a chart like the one pictured above.

For example, let's say during a given period of time the price of Bitcoin rose from $200 to $2,000 before falling to $700. A technical analyst would look at this information and determine that in the past whenever Bitcoin had risen and fallen between those three points, it ended up rising again around 100% of the time; or that there is a greater than 50% chance that this pattern will repeat itself in future periods. This information can be used to make predictions about the likely future price patterns and behavior of markets.

What does this mean for cryptocurrency investors? Theoretically, if one were able to accurately predict future market behavior based on past events, they could potentially make a lot of money. In the last five years alone, many investors have made millions off of their ability to correctly predict cryptocurrency price movements.

One could use technical analysis to identify when a coin is undervalued and buy it in the hopes that its value will eventually increase, or, when a coin is overvalued, sell it in hopes that its price will fall (if you have done your research carefully enough and understand why its value has increased or decreased).

THREE BASIC CONCEPTS OF TECHNICAL ANALYSIS

There are three basic concepts to remember when using the tools of technical analysis. These concepts are useful for making accurate predictions regarding future price movements.

#1: History Does Not Repeat Itself, But It Rhymes

The first concept is that while history may not repeat itself, it does tend to rhyme. This means that if you were able to correctly predict what would happen last month under similar circumstances, your likelihood of doing so again this month increases due to the similarities between the two situations.

#2: Market Sentiment

The second concept is that prices are heavily influenced by market sentiment. This refers to the opinions and emotions of cryptocurrency traders about a coin. If more people are bullish about a coin, its price is likely to rise as demand increases. Likewise, if more people are bearish on a coin, its price is likely to fall as demand decreases.

#3: Trends

The third concept is the importance of trends. A trend occurs when enough people begin doing something or believe something consistently over time in a way that affects the prices of assets. This concept is particularly important for investors to understand.

The idea is that if you are able to understand the general "trend" of a coin, you can use this knowledge to predict what the price will do in future periods. For example, the chart below shows a downward trend (red line) that occurred over a two-week period. If you were able to identify and predict this trend early on, you could have taken advantage of it by short selling (selling coins that you don't own with the belief that their price will fall). This trend would have allowed you to make a large profit when the price fell shortly thereafter.

WHY DO YOU NEED TECHNICAL ANALYSIS FOR CRYPTOCURRENCY INVESTMENT?

Technical analysis is not something that can be used alone to make investment decisions, but it does represent valuable information if you are looking for a better way to understand the market. It's more useful for investors who actually want to put in the time and effort required to learn its concepts than it is for casual traders or speculators.

Investors who approach investing from a macro perspective are more likely to appreciate technical analysis, whereas those who have a micro-level outlook on the market will find it unnecessary or perhaps even harmful.

WHAT TYPE OF TECHNICAL ANALYSIS IS BEST FOR CRYPTO INVESTING?

There are many different types of technical analysis. These include:

- **Fundamental analysis:** This involves looking at a coin's fundamentals in order to predict future price movements. Fundamental analysis is helpful for those who don't want to spend much time learning about charting and technical analysis, but it does require investors to perform extensive research on project fundamentals before making an investment decision.
- **Quantamental analysis:** This involves using quantitative and qualitative techniques to determine future price behavior. It uses a combination of traditional fundamental factors like the size of the circulating supply and market cap along with other data such as volatility, trading volume, and interest on social media platforms like Reddit and Twitter.
- **Cyclical analysis:** This kind of analysis focuses on the cycles within trends and how they affect prices. It is used to determine where the current cycle is in relation to historical cycles in order to predict where the price will go next.

17 / BASIC TECHNICAL ANALYSIS TOOLS FOR CRYPTOCURRENCY

THERE ARE many different tools available that you can use to carry out technical analysis. Technical analysis is a technique used to evaluate securities by analyzing statistics from the share's past prices, in order to forecast its potential future performance. In this article, we're going to go over some of the most basic technical analysis tools for cryptocurrency. We'll go through what each tool does and show examples of how you can use it for your own projects. Let's kick things off with moving averages, one of the most commonly used indicators that allows you to trade more efficiently by indicating when a trend is about to change direction.

SIMPLE MOVING AVERAGE

The simple moving average takes the sum of prices over a certain period of time and then divides it by the number of possible occurrences. For example, if you want to find the simple moving average for Bitcoin, you need to add up all

Bitcoin prices from January 1st 2016, divide that by 365 days in a year (2016 days) as well as by 8 months (240 days).

Moving averages are great for identifying trends. You interpret the direction of the trend based on where the line is located on your chart. If it's above, then the trend is upward; if it's below, a vice versa. You also look at how long it has been below or above that line for visual confirmation. Moving averages are also a good way to set support and resistance levels. For example, when the price of an asset starts falling below its moving average, it's a bearish indication of future performance. Since you're expecting the price to fall further, you might want to consider buying on those dips (or shorting) an asset and this would be a good support level where the price tends to rebound upwards.

CANDLESTICK CHARTS

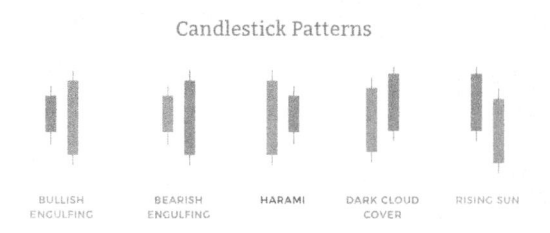

Candlestick Patterns

| BULLISH ENGULFING | BEARISH ENGULFING | HARAMI | DARK CLOUD COVER | RISING SUN |

Candlesticks are a type of financial chart used in technical analysis. They allow you to see the high, low, close, and the opening price for a given period of time. The body of the candle indicates whether the candle is Bullish or Bearish. A long bottom wick indicates that the closing price was lower than the open price and demonstrates a bearish sentiment while a long upper wick indicates that it was higher than the open and shows bullish sentiment.

SWING CHART

Swing charts are created by plotting two moving averages on top of each other. We plot one short term MA (20) on top of another SMMA (200). The distance between the two lines indicates the volatility. A large distance indicates high price action and a small distance shows low action making it easier to spot trends. You can use this technical indicator for entries and exits (when the price line crosses above or below) as a signal to go long or short.

BOLLINGER BANDS

Bollinger Bands provide another valuable tool to help you identify trends. Bollinger bands consist of three lines: middle line (MA), upper band, and lower band. Whenever the price is increasing, it will touch the upper Bollinger band, and when it's decreasing, it will hit the lower Bollinger band. After hitting, it will come back within the Bollinger's band. This is something you can use to spot trends.

BOLLINGER BAND WIDTH

Bollinger Bands demonstrate volatility by widening when volatility increases and narrowing when volatility decreases. When the price hits the upper or lower bands, it is a significant and important point to take note of.

MONKEY

The monkey indicator demonstrates a graphical way to find support levels and resistance levels. For example, when the price of Bitcoin has increasing volume on a given day, that indicates that the price is going to increase substantially (even all-time high). If the volume on a particular day exceeds preceding days, this means there was more activity in that day, and it could potentially bring in better opportunities for your investments.

OSCILLATORS

Oscillators are used to predict the momentum of an asset price. They're represented with a graph that shows the trend of an asset's performance in a certain time period. MACD (moving average convergence divergence), Stochastic Oscillator, RSI (relative strength index) are examples of oscillators you can use to perform technical analysis. Quotes or tickers such as BTCUSD, ETHBTC, LTCUSD, DASHBTC, XRPETH are some examples that you can look at what is going on in the markets and get better understanding of what's happening with your investments.

MFI (MONEY FLOW INDICES)

Money flow indicators are used to identify trends in market psychology. They indicate the inflow and outflow of money. A price chart with an MFI below 0 shows more money going out of the market than coming in, whereas a price chart with an MFI above 0 shows more money coming into the market than leaving it. An MFI of 20 would be equivalent to $20,000 worth of Bitcoins being traded every minute, while an MFI below 20 would indicate that $5000 worth of Bitcoins are traded per minute. MFI can be used to identify the market sentiment in a visual way. The logical thing that it tells you is if the price of something increases/decreases, then there must be more people buying/selling. As a result, the price increases/decrease. Money Flow Index is similar to Moving averages in that it can show you the trend of an asset.

MOMENTUM

The momentum of any asset can be seen by looking at its momentum indicators such as RSI (relative strength index). For example, during periods when RSI is high, this indicates that there is a lot of buying pressure and vice versa for low RSI values.

At a glance, Relative Strength Indicator (RSI) can tell you whether your investment is trending up or down and also if it is highly volatile. If the value of RSI is between 30 to 60, it means that the price movement is slowly rising and that there is little steepness to the current price action. When RSI values are between 0 and 30, it indicates a strong downward trend. On the other hand, when the RSI values are above 70, it indicates an upward trend where prices are going up and usually very quickly.

TRACTION

Traction refers to how much trading activity takes place in a particular currency. Traction is usually measured using trading volume. A high trading volume suggests a higher level of interest and activity in a given currency. You can see traction in exchanges such as Coinbase, Poloniex, Bitfinex, Kukoin, or other exchanges that have a market of cryptocurrencies in your region.

SWING HIGHS/LOWS

Swing Highs and Swings Lows are the high price and low price over the past few days or week. The first swing high is the highest price reached during the period while the second swing high indicates the new level of highs on that chart.

18 / CRYPTOCURRENCY AND TAXES

CRYPTOCURRENCY CAN BE A CONFUSING, if not daunting, topic to wrap one's mind around. Competing theoretical frameworks and dense terminology abound, making it hard for those without a background in the myriad of disciplines that encompass the field. Even ordinary laypersons can have difficulty understanding the topic; and yet, it is likely that, soon enough, states will begin to attempt to tax numerous areas of cryptocurrency use.

I believe it is difficult - if not impossible - for states to fairly tax cryptocurrencies. Cryptocurrencies are created via complex mathematical processes known as mining; they are issued or "mined" by individuals who use powerful computers to find them; and they exist on a decentralized electronic ledger.

IS CRYPTOCURRENCY TAXABLE?

The query of whether or not cryptocurrencies will be taxed is a difficult one to answer. After all, it is unclear whether or not they should be considered a currency, an asset, or a commodity.

Under US law, cryptos are deemed to be property and therefore liable to capital gains tax. However this is only paid at the point at which gains are realized and earned as income when you decide to sell.It is not hard to see why the IRS would view them this way. If a buyer pays for goods or services with a cryptocurrency, he/she could be considered to have sold his/her cryptocurrency in exchange for the good or service. Thus, a taxable gain would result. Furthermore, if one were to hold cryptocurrencies over time, selling them for more than one paid for them (regardless of whether they are paid up front or on credit), a capital gain would occur as well.

These two examples are somewhat simple: at least in theory, it is possible to determine what price the original owner paid and what price it was sold for when paying with cryptocurrencies - even if there is no physical fiat currency involved in the transaction.

The situation becomes more difficult, however, when one considers how the IRS defines and treats barter. In general, barter must be reported when the value of what is received exceeds the value of what was given up.

So, let's say that someone uses his/her cryptocurrency to pay a mechanic $500 for a repair. The mechanic then uses his/her cryptocurrency to pay his/her electric bill. This would be a taxable event because it is not clear whether or not the mechanic received more or less than what he/she gave up; this is particularly true if the cryptocurrency's value has increased in the interim since it was used to pay for repairs.

The situation becomes even more complicated when one considers that cryptocurrency is sold for a wide variety of goods and services. Not only does the mechanic have to consider what price he/she received for the repair, but also the price he/she paid for goods and services from a number of other third parties. Anyone who accepts payment in cryptocurrency can become a tax nexus.

It is important to note that this situation is not unique to cryptocurrency; barter transactions have existed since time immemorial and they are still taxable. The IRS treats barter as taxable because it is treated like currency: when two people exchange goods without using money, they still need an agreed-upon medium of exchange to determine value (i.e., they essentially price in the money they would have used had they actually been trading with cash).

Traditionally, barter has been difficult to regulate because it is difficult to track. After all, there is no actual exchange of cash. Thus, tax authorities are forced to use a "totaling" method of accounting: they total the value of what was paid and the value of what was received - and tax the difference.

LAWS ABOUT TAXES IN CRYPTOCURRENCY

Tax authorities, of course, are required to fill their coffers with money to fund government operations. Irrespective of what may or may not be dictated by principles of fairness, cryptocurrency will likely be under to taxation at some point in the near future. This is not necessarily a bad thing. After all, this will help states fund important government programs and it will help prevent citizens from evading taxes.

Not every state can be the first to pass cryptocurrency-specific legislation due to slow bureaucratic processes — and also because some states would rather wait for other states to set an example that they can follow rather than take a risk by trying something innovative. It is a problematic condition to navigate, but I believe that states should wait for guidance from the IRS before proceeding.

The laws of the United States are federal, and the federal government (rather than state or local authorities) issues tax regulations and outlines tax policy. Thus, we must look to Washington in order to determine what the correct legal framework is for taxation of cryptocurrency. It should be distinguished that, in many cases, state law mirrors federal law, -so states will likely follow suit.

I believe that the long-term trend will be toward treating cryptocurrencies as property.

19 / EXCHANGE MARKETS IN CRYPTOCURRENCY

CRYPTOCURRENCY EXCHANGE

A CRYPTOCURRENCY EXCHANGE is a trading platform or marketplace where traders can trade cryptocurrencies. They allow buy and sell orders to be matched for exchange goods, like stocks, but binaries are usually used for crypto-based markets.

The first crypto currency ever traded on an exchange was Bitcoin. The exchanges were a way to generate liquidity in the trading of Bitcoins — with their increasing popularity, they also function as market makers for fast trade execution and price discovery. There are even platforms that allow the creation of metacoins and tokens that have had their own value created by the demand for them.

The largest Bitcoin exchange as of December 2017 has been Japan-based bitFlyer.

ALGORITHM-BASED TRADING

Algorithm-based trading is an extremely popular form of trading in this market. Algorithms allow traders to program their own strategies and execute trades at will. Trade execution itself is a hot topic, with high frequency trading bots taking advantage of tiny changes in price. The automated nature of the crypto markets means that human emotion cannot get involved in the sentiment of the market, creating a historically rational environment for outside traders to take advantage of. Bots have already been implemented by many traders, both professional and amateur alike.

The company Quantopian uses a platform called Zipline, which is based on the Python programming language, to create automated algorithmic traders. It is used by both professionals and amateurs alike.

Cryptocurrency trading bots are very controversial in that they can allow inexperienced traders to enter into cryptocurrency markets and simply purchase at will without understanding the fundamentals behind the price movement of cryptocurrencies. This could result in massive losses for those who do not understand what they are doing.

LIQUIDITY

Liquidity is a very important factor for any market, but is especially crucial with cryptocurrencies. The liquidity of the trading platform decides how easy it will be to get rid of your coins in a bad market without losing significant value. If this liquidity is low, selling could become impossible if there are no buyers at your offer price. This is why an exchange that has the same strict regulations and standards as other popular stock exchanges can have a major advantage over other exchanges.

The liquidity of a cryptocurrency exchange will heavily influence its price movements because of the volume of buyers and sellers on its platform. The more people are willing to buy or sell prices off from the real market value, the more volatile an exchange becomes. This is because the exchange will not be reflective of the true value of its underlying assets, so it will become much more volatile.

However, with the more popular exchanges, this should not be much of a problem because professional traders and companies that have a lot to gain from crypto prices can trade on that exchange and ensure liquidity.

Liquidity is also important for exiting a position because of the speed in which you can do it at any time. A cryptocurrency exchange with low liquidity will take longer to exit a trade and as such, increase your risk exposure during that time period.

Some exchanges will use different order types or variations of existing order types to give an advantage to different kinds of traders. Traders may find certain order types more useful than others depending on the kind of market conditions.

MARKET ORDERS

Market orders are used when trades are executed without any certainty as to what price will be obtained. Buy or sell orders for a cryptocurrency will lead to an instant trading of that coin at the best price currently on the exchange.

LIMIT ORDER

A limit order is placed when a trader wishes to buy or sell a cryptocurrency at a specific price or better. This allows for more certainty in trading and removes some of the uncertainty from the cryptocurrency markets. Whilst it may seem counterintuitive to place trade restrictions, it actually makes sense given how volatile these markets can be - more experienced traders should look into this further.

An example of a limit order is placing a sell order for Bitcoin at a price of $5,000 when the current market rate is $5,250. This will ensure higher trading volumes when the price reaches this level.

STOP ORDER

Stop orders are used to stop losses from becoming any worse. If the value of an asset drops to below a certain price level, then a trade will be executed automatically. This feature can be useful when markets start turning downward in which it could lead to significant losses if left unchecked.

A stop loss is used to cut losses short and ensure that they are only losing as much as they intended due to a sudden spike downwards in prices.

The benefit of stop losses is that they can protect users in a sudden downward market when most other traders are not yet aware of it.

A trailing stop loss is used to ensure that the loss does not increase any further. This is useful when cryptocurrency prices are rapidly dropping because users want to ensure that their portfolio doesn't lose any further than it has already on the dip. It essentially stops an exchange from losing any more money when the price starts moving upwards again.

Stop orders can be used as entry or exit points for positions to give flexibility in how users trade cryptocurrencies.

MARGIN TRADING

Margin trading is another interesting concept thatt can be done through some cryptocurrency exchanges. This allows users to trade with more than they actually have in their exchange wallet. The amount of margin that can be applied to a trade can range from 50% to 1,000% depending on the exchange.

A bit like leverage on traditional stock markets, this allows traders to open positions much larger than they could fund, although these trades will be at a higher risk because of the exposure that they have towards the underlying asset.

This can be useful for some traders to speculate and make higher rewards on their trades. However, it should be noted that margin trading creates a lot of risk for users because of the leverage and speculative nature associated with it.

Cryptocurrency exchanges are not like a regular stock exchange where prices of shares are based on strict regulations and standards. Therefore, this can make them more prone to manipulation and price volatility. This is especially true when volumes are low so the market makers at crypto exchanges often have an ability to manipulate prices at will.

It is because of these factors that some people consider cryptocurrency exchanges as being a risky business where there is little security for your account or assets.

IDENTITY CHECK

There are a few features that all cryptocurrency exchanges have in common. Firstly, you will have to register with an email address and password before you can start using the exchange. This is to ensure that each person has one account and is not impersonating somebody else.

This is a requirement of most cryptocurrency exchanges because they want every user to be identified, but some do not take this process very seriously. There are also cases of where registered accounts are simply taken over through phishing or other various techniques, which can sometimes lead to identity theft.

However, there are also some exchanges that allow for anonymous trading using a cryptocurrency such as Dash. This is often the case on decentralized exchanges, and it requires a different approach.

In general, most exchanges will require that users submit an official bank statement or identification document to verify their identity. This will usually take between 1-5 days before your account is activated and you are able to start trading on the platform.

The registration process of cryptocurrency exchanges can

be very time consuming compared to other regulated financial institutions. Some don't even allow for users in certain countries to interact with their platforms which can pose as another setback for some traders.

This also means that some cryptocurrency exchanges have higher fees because they must pay for more expensive licensing amongst other overheads that may not be applicable at crypto-to-crypto exchange platforms.

To conclude, the process of registering with cryptocurrency exchanges may vary but they are all necessary measures to ensure that users are committed to their trading. There are a few other verifications processes you may need to go through after signing up such as internal and external audits.

It is also important to note that the registration process is not always one-sided. In some cases, users can open an account without having their identity verified by the exchange. This means that users often have to take extra precautions in order to keep their assets safe and secure from other users on the platform.

20 / COMMONLY USED TERMS IN CRYPTOCURRENCY AND THEIR DEFINITIONS

HERE IS a list of most commonly used term in cryptocurrency and its meaning.

- *Bitcoin.* Bitcoin is a digital currency that's not tied to any national government and enables faster, cheaper payments to anyone in the world. Bitcoin can also be traded like you would trade stocks. Bitcoin was the first blockchain coin, which means it's the most popular one around thus far.
- *Blockchain.* The blockchain is a public ledger of all Bitcoin transactions that have ever been executed. It also serves as a distributed database of that information, making it decentralized.
- *Cryptocurrency.* Cryptocurrencies are digital currencies that are encrypted for security or that otherwise resist counterfeiting. The first and most popular cryptocurrency is Bitcoin. Other popular

cryptocurrencies include Ethereum, Litecoin, Ripple, and Dash.
- *Mining.* Mining is the act of securing transactions in a particular cryptocurrency by solving mathematical puzzles. This process will also generate new crypto coins that can be saved for future use or traded with other users for goods or services offered through that blockchain platform.
- *Fiat currency.* Fiat currencies are regulated by government bodies such as the Federal Reserve System in the US, which issues dollars and requires commercial banks to follow its rules (including providing dollars when required). This is different from decentralized digital currencies like Bitcoin that are issued through mining processes (see below).
- *Transaction fee/miner fees/transaction costs.* The cost to make a transaction in a particular cryptocurrency is called the transaction fee or miner fee. These fees are paid to the miners who use their computer power to approve and record transactions on the blockchain. They are expected to verify whether the sender of the funds has that much money available in his/her account.
- *Decentralized/Centralized.* Decentralization means there is no central authority that controls a particular currency; all the processing is done by users or nodes on that network, which means there are no centralized points of failure (i.e., no one can shut down your system).

- *Ledger/Blockchain/Digital ledger.* The blockchain is a digital ledger of transactions that are recorded chronologically and publicly.
- *Tokens/Coins.* Platform-specific cryptocurrencies created by a blockchain project team in the form of an ICO (Initial Coin Offering). For example, if you invested in Ethereum's ICO, you got Ether tokens in exchange.
- *Assets and cryptocurrency values.* Cryptocurrency values are closely linked to asset classes like stocks, bonds, real estate, etc., which have been developed as a means to invest and store value for many years now. Cryptocurrencies are still in their infancy but already have shown to be a more volatile investment than stocks.
- *Wallet/Blockchain Wallet/Digital Wallets*: A cryptocurrency wallet is a piece of software that stores your private and public keys. Private keys are like the PIN to withdraw cash from your bank account. Without them, you can't access your money (in this case, cryptocurrency). As such, it's vital you keep them protected. Public keys are used by others to send funds or by yourself when sending funds.
- *Cold storage Cold storage wallet:* This is the safest method of storing your cryptocurrency. Typically, you'll use a paper wallet in conjunction with a USB-hardware wallet to store your cryptocurrency offline. See also: Hardware Wallet.
- *DApp:* Decentralized applications that run on a

P2P network of computers, kind of like the internet (see Appendix: Crypto Acronyms). Ethereum is one of the best-known platforms for DApps.

- *Blockchain Explorer/Explorer/Block Explorer:* A blockchain explorer is similar to an internet search engine that mines and indexes transaction data from open blockchains. These explorers offer valuable insights and analytics about transactions in past blocks, which are stored on the blockchain forever.
- *ICO:* An initial coin offering is a first sale of a cryptocurrency token to investors. Often this takes the form of a digital asset, so that it's easier to transfer between buyers and sellers and even trade on secondary markets. It's like an IPO — Initial Public Offering — but for cryptocurrencies.
- *Fork:* A fork occurs when a cryptocurrency splits into two different coins. Forks can happen when a cryptocurrency developer becomes unhappy with the current development path of a coin and isn't able to convince other developers to come on board with his/her ideas. They are often referred to as "hard forks" and "soft forks." Hard forks result in two different cryptocurrencies with separate blockchains, while soft forks typically only create one new cryptocurrency option.
- *Changelly/Shapeshift/Decentralized exchanges:* Changelly and ShapeShift are services that enable you to exchange one crypto asset for another

(thereby avoiding an increase in fees). Both of these services run on top of a decentralized exchange (DEX). Different from a centralized exchange, which requires you to deposit funds with an exchange and wait for them to handle the transactions for you, decentralized exchanges don't have access to your money. So-called smart contracts enable trading without depositing or withdrawing funds.

- *Mining.* Mining cryptocurrency is similar to mining gold, except the tools to mine are much more sophisticated and costly. Normally, it requires a significant investment in hardware (e.g., GPUs) and electricity. Miners are rewarded for their work by the network, but they also have to compete with other miners who want to solve the next block of transactions at any given time.
- *PoW/Proof of Work/Hash rate*: Proof-of-Work requires high-performance systems and high energy costs for mining new coins. It's also known as proof of work, or PoW, and it was pioneered by Bitcoin. Proof of Stake (PoS) is a type of algorithm for achieving distributed consensus through requesting users to show ownership of a certain amount of currency before being allowed to participate in network consensus. PoS is an alternative to the PoW algorithm, which is used by Bitcoin and many other cryptocurrencies.
- *Fee/Miner fee:* When you send transactions, miners prioritize these transactions using complex

mathematical formulas. The first miner to solve the problem gets rewarded with cryptocurrency, and all subsequent transactions take longer to process since other miners have to solve their own problems in order to win cryptocurrency rewards. This means that if you want your transaction processed quickly, you'll have to pay a higher miner fee.

AFTERWORD

Cryptocurrency is still very new, and there is a lot left to be discovered about how it will affect our future. But it's important to remember that cryptocurrency, and the blockchain technology that makes it possible, was created for one single purpose: enabling people across the world to transact with each other without a middleman.

That means more autonomy for everyone, more privacy in our transactions, and more freedom in our transactions than any of us have had before. It also means no arbitrary limits on the number of coins you can own—or spend—at any time.

This is an idea that everyone should be able to get behind. Why should you have to ask anyone's permission before sending money to your family or friends? Why should you wait days for a transaction to process before being able to use your money? Why should the government be able to monitor and control how you spend your hard-earned cash?

Cryptocurrency is, above all else, focused on freedom. And it will only work if we all stick together and fight against the powers that try to suppress that freedom. We may not win every time, but over time, we can win more battles than we lose. And eventually, the world will see just how much better cryptocurrency really is—and join us in making it a reality.

Here are some more practical tips in investing to cryptocurrency:

1. Invest only what you can afford to lose. In this way, you can focus more on the investment and less on the money.
2. The newer coins are usually riskier than the older ones, i.e., Bitcoin is safer than Ethereum and Ethereum is safer than NEO.
3. Choose coins with a strong community backing them up; check their social media pages and team members' background (see below).
4. Always research about the coin before investing in them: visit their website, read their whitepaper, check out their GitHub repository for development activity or see if they have open-source code available on GitHub.
5. Always be updated with crypto news/updates via Facebook groups and other social media.
6. Stay sober and patient, and don't be the one to panic sell in the market's dip!
7. Don't just follow a cryptocurrency's price trend; study their technology, team members,

partnerships, etc., too. This will help you determine if the coin has real-world use cases.
8. Buy low, sell high! This is pretty self-explanatory so I won't elaborate much here... But hey, some investors actually do this by buying when a coin is down in price and selling it when it has become super hyped up and reached its all-time high.
9. Pick a project/coin you believe in, not just one that will make you money.
10. Do your own research and take responsibility for your actions (you hear this a lot, perhaps because it is important).
11. Avoid pump and dump scams. There are a lot of them out there, where people intentionally spread false information or enthusiastically talk up something to make it seem like an amazing opportunity only to sell once the price is pumped up or down so far, the value has completely changed (often completely destroyed). Remember, if it sounds too good to be true, it probably is.

I hope that this book had helped you to have a bit of an insight of what cryptocurrency is and the future of its technology as well. I strongly recommend you to continue your research on Bitcoin and the other cryptocurrencies because it is an evolving market, and even if these are the best tips in investing to cryptocurrency, they might not work for you! Be open-minded and focus on technologies that will help you grow your money!

With these ideas in mind, we can walk into the future

with our heads held up high... knowing that we'll always be free to transact with whoever we want, whenever we want, however we want—without asking anyone for permission.

See you around, buddy!

ACKNOWLEDGMENTS

Loving thanks to my wife, Suzanne, for her total support and being a book widow with such good grace. To L. Austen Johnson who cared enough to read the manuscript and to make insightful and telling suggestions, serving as editor and designer to produce the book you now hold and hopefully enjoy. I am more grateful than I can say.

ABOUT THE AUTHOR

Ian Ellul is a writer and technology expert with over twenty-five years of experience exploring the intersection of technology and communications. He lives in the United Kingdom, where he continues to act as a quality assurance manager for companies like FedEx and Inspired Energy. His extensive background in the industry allows him to write about new technologies like blockchain and cryptocurrencies with an expert's hand, making them both deeply informative and easy-to-understand. He has held his own investment in a portfolio of alt-coins since 2019, which has since grown by 1138%. *Cracking the Code to Cryptocurrency Investments* is his first book.

Made in the USA
Monee, IL
27 May 2021